THE OLD INNS OF ENGLAND

'HERITAGE' BOOKS

Published or in Preparation

Uniform with this Volume   7s. 6d. net each

———

THE CATHEDRALS OF ENGLAND
By HARRY BATSFORD and CHARLES FRY

ENGLISH VILLAGES
By the Hon. HUMPHREY PAKINGTON

THE FACE OF SCOTLAND
By HARRY BATSFORD and CHARLES FRY
Second Edition

THE HEART OF SCOTLAND
By GEORGE BLAKE

Published by
B. T. BATSFORD LTD
15 North Audley Street, London, W.1

I   THE SPREAD EAGLE, WITHAM, ESSEX

*From a Water Colour
by Randolph Schwabe*

THE OLD INNS
OF ENGLAND

By

A. E. RICHARDSON
F.S.A., F.R.I.B.A.

With a foreword by
SIR EDWIN LUTYENS, R.A.

Illustrated from drawings by
BRIAN COOK
and from photographs

LONDON
B. T. BATSFORD LTD
15 NORTH AUDLEY STREET, W.1

DEDICATION
TO THE STEWARDS AND MEMBERS
OF THE JOCKEY CLUB
NEWMARKET, 1934

First Published, June 1934

MADE AND PRINTED IN GREAT BRITAIN
FOR THE PUBLISHERS, B. T. BATSFORD LTD., LONDON
TEXT BY UNWIN BROTHERS LTD., WOKING
PLATES BY THE DARIEN PRESS, EDINBURGH

FOREWORD

By Sir EDWIN LUTYENS, R.A.

There can be little that inspires a reminiscent imagination more than the history of the old Inns of England, which, through centuries, have waved their signs of open welcome to all who passed their way; and wherein men of all classes met to pass the time of day and to exchange views on matters of immediate interest: great names, perhaps, unwitting each of the other's identity.

The invention of the railways and the growth of their great systems left the roadway Inns to desultory neglect. Now, the giant growth of motors and of motorists has brought our old roads, and the Inns adorning them, into a renewed existence.

The new roads demand new Inns, and may they, too, wave their signs of welcome to those who travel along them, and carry on, in their building, the great traditions of our national architecture.

Much good work is being done, but there are regrettable exceptions, such as the adjectival 'olde worlde' creations, which are as objectionable and as needless as are the ultra-modern, in that both deface our countryside.

It is not possible to replace or displace old traditions in the twinkling of an eye. Tradition is quite admirably shown in this book.

There is no doubt but that the Brewers and the great Industries catering for our need realise the importance of the service that is theirs to render, and it is amazing, in these days, that their work should be hindered and hampered by Act of Parliament bearing the initials that can but justly relate to some dotty old woman, D.O.R.A.

Surely the responsible men of business and of affairs of this our England know how to run their houses for the comfort of their patrons, without outside interference. They know, too, that a good name in public service is one of too great a value to lose by ill-fame and by a lack of that cleanliness, moral and physical, that pertains to all that is good.

PREFACE

When Mr. Batsford approached me with the suggestion for a new book on the Inns, I felt a certain hesitation in undertaking it, for the subject had already been treated as exhaustively as seemed to me possible in my own and Mr. Eberlein's *English Inn, Past and Present*, published in 1925 and now out of print. This volume was planned on the ample scale possible before the Depression, and issued with success at the then moderate price of a guinea. But the guinea book, I am told by my publishers, for good or ill, is a thing of the past, and to compile anything approaching a representative pictorial survey at the present cheap price has involved a very rigorous discipline, not only as regards the choice of photographs, but in the planning of the letterpress itself. In this latter it has been difficult to avoid, in several aspects of the subject, a certain amount of repetition of earlier facts and statements, but the reader may rest assured that every endeavour has been made to present a new treatment; the arrangement is on entirely original lines, and the whole work has gained enormously from some nine years of fresh reading and constant travel about the country. In particular, I feel that the inclusion of a long chapter on "The Inn in Literature," with excerpts from the English authors from Langland to Surtees, will prove a thoroughly welcome innovation.

The illustrations, I think, can be left to speak for themselves, but a comparison with my earlier book will reveal the remarkable advances made in the art and technique of photography during those intervening years. As regards their choice, an effort has been made to season the array of famous and indispensable examples with some personal discoveries that I believe are not generally familiar to the public, and at the same time to represent every degree of English Inn, from the 'Baby Austin' to the 'Rolls Royce,' with some reference to usage and situation, and not forgetful of such familiar types as the riverside fishing inn, the great inn of county town or cathedral city, the hedgeside alehouse, the snug refuge on wind-swept moors or heights, and, above all, the neat and comfortable village hostelry, which so far outnumbers the other categories, and is of all most characteristic of the tranquil English landscape. As a field of illustration it is unending; and it is to be hoped that these examples, carefully chosen out of a mass of fine material, will serve to kindle the imagination of the reader, bucolic or otherwise, to keep a more watchful eye on his travels, for these fine survivals of old English life and architecture, which, in their un-ostentatious way, provide as interesting a study as the churches, the manor-houses, or the castles, and express perfectly the sober trend of English vernacular building through some five centuries.

In conclusion, I should like to thank Professor Randolph Schwabe for the delightful frontispiece, specially executed for this work; Mr. Brian Cook, who has provided the pen-and-ink drawings and the spirited jacket; and Sir Edwin Lutyens for his characteristically stimulating Foreword.

A. E. R.

AMPTHILL,
June 1934.

ACKNOWLEDGMENT

The publishers must acknowledge their obligation to the band of photographers whose work is reproduced in these pages, namely, Mr. Herbert Felton for Figs. 4, 9, 10, 21, 25, 29, 30, 37, 42, 45, 47, 51, 52, 53, 60, 62, 63, 64, 65, 66, 73, 77–81, 85, 87, 91, 93, 94, 99, 100, 106–110, 113, 118, 125, 127, 128; Messrs. F. Frith & Co., of Reigate, for Fig. 56; Mr. Bernard Griffin, of Dorchester, for Fig. 22; Mr. E. O. Hoppé for Figs. 82, 122; Mr. Donald McLeish for Figs. 43, 44, 68, 70, 71; Mr. J. Dixon Scott for Figs. 8, 13, 14, 17, 36, 39–41, 50, 57, 72, 76, 97, 123; and Mr. Will F. Taylor for Figs. 2, 3, 5–7, 11, 12, 15, 16, 18–20, 23, 24, 26–28, 31, 32, 34, 35, 38, 46, 49, 54, 55, 58, 59, 61, 67, 69, 74, 75, 83, 84, 86, 88, 89, 90, 92, 95, 96, 98, 101–105, 111, 112, 114–117, 119–121, 124, 126, 129–132. The colour illustrations of the Elizabethan frieze at *The White Swan*, Stratford-on-Avon (Figs. 105 A, B), are included by courtesy of Messrs. Trust Houses, Ltd., the illustration on page 59 is reproduced by permission of the Director and Secretary of the Victoria and Albert Museum from a drawing by Basil Oliver, F.R.I.B.A., and the end-papers are reproduced from coloured prints after James Pollard in the collections of Mr. L. F. R. Coote, A.R.I.B.A., and of the Author.

CONTENTS

2 THE BELL, HURLEY, BERKSHIRE. The gabled inn of a
Thameside village

3 THE BELL, STILTON, HUNTINGDONSHIRE   A fine early
coaching inn on the Great North Road.

THE OLD INNS OF ENGLAND

I

THE INN AND THE ROAD

If, to you, 'Saloon' is different from 'Public Bar,' and both are different from 'Jug and Bottle': if you know better than to order beer in a Wine House: if you can feel the difference between 'coffee-room' and 'restaurant': if you would rather have a quick one leaning against a bar, with your feet on a sawdust floor, than sitting on a hard fake-Tudor chair, at a shiny fake-Plantagenet table, with a disinfected fake-marble floor beneath you and a spiky palm above your head: if you are the sort of person who does not get shown into the parlour as soon as you enter a village alehouse: then this book is intended for you.

If, on the other hand, you use the roads just as a means of transit from one town to another: if you really think that sham medieval beams on the outside of a large and obviously new public-house are preferable to no decoration at all, beyond the good proportions of windows, and honest stone or bricks: if 'de luxe' attracts you more than 'family and commercial': if you think that true comfort and civilisation are somehow connected with the words 'up to date': then you have no business to have read this book beyond the opening paragraphs. For we are not dealing with palatial hotels, but with inns large and small.

Now most inns, whatever their size, are the centre of the town. They are the homes of gossip and political opinion, from which issue forth plans for local sports and slate-club subscriptions. The social grades in an inn, the local customs and games in the bar, are surrounded by a ritual and taboo as complicated as an elaborate church service. The inn as a social centre has never been studied closely enough. Before all the old people who fill up a bar on a Saturday evening die off, perhaps the significance of the inn will be studied and chronicled by some economists and psychologists.

The story of the inn is a long and complex one, running like a thread through the social history of some seven or eight centuries, inextricably connected with the wayfaring life and the restless traffic of the English roads. Before the fourteenth century there had only been inns in the larger towns such as London, with a sprinkling of taverns and wayside alehouses along the highways. In parishes much frequented by pilgrims and other travellers, special

A MEDIEVAL GALLERIED INN-YARD, FORMERLY AT ST. ALBANS
(NOW DEMOLISHED)

guest-houses were often established by the Church or the Lord of the Manor; and of these the Church House at Holne, in Devon, and *The Pilgrims' Inn* at Glastonbury (4), are famous examples. At such houses the charges were beyond the purses of any but the well-to-do, though there were often annexes for poor people, which were probably little more than timber sheds, with rush-strewn floors, a brazier, and some crude furniture consisting of wooden benches and a long table. The principal hospitality was still provided by the monasteries, and it was not until the dominant influence of the Church in social life began to decline that the inn really established itself as a national institution.

Outside the towns, the English inns grew up along the roads, and were to be found at convenient halting-places such as villages, cross-roads, and ferries. Here the accommodation would be rough and limited, often consisting of no more than a common dormitory. The buildings were generally infested, rats and mice ran wild among the rushes of the floor, and the bedding, in which the travellers slept naked in the fashion of the time, was as likely as not verminous, as indeed it often continued to be in the smaller and out-of-the-way inns until after Pepys' day. Ale was the national beverage, and this was universally provided at meals, and could be obtained at roadside houses which displayed the sign of an evergreen bush attached to a projecting pole (p. 50). The peasantry congregated at these taverns, as also did robbers, quacks, mountebanks, and undesirables of every kind and of both sexes. London particularly was famed for its taverns of good and ill repute, and in the fourteenth century the licence existing in these places had reached such a pitch that the King forbade the keeping of open house after Curfew (much as modern authority closes down our own respectable establishments at ten o'clock) "because such offenders as aforesaid, going about by night, do commonly resort and have their meetings and hold their evil talk in taverns more than elsewhere, and there do seek for shelter, lying in wait and watching their time to do mischief." Langland's description of tavern company is expressive:—

Thomme the tynkere, and tweye of his knaves,
Hicke the hackenyman, and Houwe the neldere,
Claryce of Cocheslane, the clerke of the churche,
An haywarde and an heremyte, the hangman of Tyborne,
Dauwe the dykere, with a dosen harlotes,
Of portours and of pyke-porses and pylede toth-drawers

Ther was lauhying and lakeryng and let go the coppe
Bargeynes and bevereges by-gunne to aryse
And seten so til evesong rank. . . .

Of the fourteenth-century inn only a few fragments

survive in the fabric of later buildings, such as the
remarkable ground-floor range of traceried windows in
The Coopers' Arms in Tilehouse Street, Hitchin, and in
all probability the vaulted cellars beneath *The Mitre* at
Oxford and *The Fleece* at Gloucester. But with the fifteenth
century the inn began to assume a new importance, for,

THE 'COOPERS' ARMS,' TILEHOUSE STREET, HITCHIN, AS IT WAS A
HUNDRED YEARS AGO (AFTER J. C. BUCKLER)

despite the social upheavals of The Wars of the Roses,
trade was on the increase, and a new merchant class
arising with whom travel became a much more frequent
necessity, largely owing to the boom in English raw wool,
which was the national industry of the Middle Ages.
The inn of the fifteenth century was conceived on a
more stately scale than anything previously attempted,
and it is a piece of good fortune that at least two great
houses have been preserved from this period, in outward

4 THE GEORGE, GLASTONBURY, SOMERSET. A fifteenth-century pilgrims' inn

5 THE ANGEL, GRANTHAM, LINCOLNSHIRE. A splendid medieval inn on the Great North Road which once lodged Richard III

6 THE FALSTAFF, CANTERBURY, KENT. A fine seventeenth-century inn, just outside the West Gate, on the site of an ancient pilgrims' hostel

appearance still largely intact. Of these, brief reference has already been made to *The Pilgrims' Inn* at Glastonbury (4), which is described in some detail in the next chapter. The other, *The Angel* at Grantham (5), is probably of even earlier date, a stately stone fabric with projecting bays to left and right, and a central archway into the yard beneath the famous oriel window resting on its carved and once gilded angel-bracket. This digni-

THE MEDIEVAL STABLE-YARD OF THE CLASSICAL 'GEORGE' AT
WEST WYCOMBE

fied frontage is all that remains of the original inn; the timber galleries, stables, and great barns of its courtyards have vanished, to be replaced by later and more permanent ranges. A number of other famous inns date largely from this period, but few are in such perfect preservation, though the lower storey of *The George* at Norton St. Philip (34), also described in the next chapter, remains largely as when it was built, beneath a superstructure added during the next century. *The George* at Bedford, *The Falstaff* at Canterbury (6), *The Fighting Cocks* at St. Albans (103), *The Star* at Alfriston (55), and

The New Inn at Gloucester (7) all incorporate much fifteenth-century work, the latter, though considerably altered, retaining the quadrangular galleried arrangement of its yard.

It is with the sixteenth century, and the settled peace of the Tudor period, that the inn first enters on its great days. In the country, though the main roads were still the same rough ways that had been frequented for centuries previously, dust-laden in the summer and almost impassable in winter, "when blood be nipt and ways be foule," travelling was far more common. This, however, was at first largely medieval in character, horseback being still preferred to journeys by waggon or palanquin. At the same time, considerable improvements were taking place in the design of saddles and pillions, and huge wheeled travelling machines were coming into use among the provincial gentry for transporting their families to London and other distant places. Towards the end of the century, wheeled carriages became much more numerous; Elizabeth herself had set the fashion on those dusty but lyrical voyages about her realm in which she delighted.

The inn now began to fulfil a definite function in social life, half public and half domestic; and the passage of the century witnessed an astonishing increase in its numbers. This increase may have been partly due to the suppression of the monasteries and consequent disappearance of their guest-houses, but there is no doubt that the new type of hostelry throve chiefly because it accorded so perfectly with the changing social system. In 1577 an Order in Council was made for a return of the exact number of inns, alehouses, and taverns throughout England, with a view to levying a tax on them towards the cost of repairing Dover Harbour. From this we learn that in Norfolk (a teeming wool county) there were 480 houses, while in Staffordshire only 105. In the thinly populated eastern and middle marches of the Scottish Borders there were 238, while in Middlesex there were no less than 876, made up of 132 inns, 24 taverns, and 720 alehouses.

In its planning the Tudor inn, though generally built

on a much larger scale, varied little from its medieval prototype, the central gateway, with its massive oak door, giving access to a galleried courtyard, with a second yard beyond for stabling and waggons, and generally another exit in the rear to a back lane for use in cases of congestion. Inside the inns themselves, however, the accommodation had improved enormously, for private bedrooms were now generally obtainable, dark wainscoted chambers, furnished with the heavy carved-oak movables of the period; and, by the reign of Elizabeth, a general posting system for the hire of horses had been established. The inventory of *The Tabard* at Southwark gives some idea of the extent and arrangement of one of the larger Elizabethan inns in any part of the country. The traveller, coming in by the central entrance, would probably turn into a large ground-floor room facing the street called 'the Darke Parlour.' Also on the ground-floor was a hall and a general reception-room called 'the Parlour,' the latter being used for meals, and having the vaulted cellars beneath it, as at *The Mitre* at Oxford. On the first floor, above the parlour and the hall, were three rooms, 'the Middle Chamber,' 'the Corner Chamber,' and 'Maister Hussye's Chamber,' with garrets, or 'cook-lofts,' above them. Other rooms were picturesquely named 'the Entry Chamber,' 'the Reine Chamber,' 'the Flower de Luce Chamber,' and 'Mr. Russell's Chamber,' while the outbuildings included a warehouse, a coal-hole, an oven-house, and privies. The kitchen appointments comprised an astonishing collection of kettles, pots, pans, and basins of brass and copper, brass candlesticks, and a stone mortar. The pothooks, tongs, mincing-mills, griddles, frying-pans, and steamers were made of Sussex iron. The pantry contained a variety of drinking vessels, including pewter pots graded from the pottle to the gill, glasses, stone utensils, and trenchers. In the provision of bed linen, great advances had been made in the equipment of the more important inns, for, by the reign of Elizabeth, the better-class traveller expected linen sheets, table-cloths, diapers, and napkins.

In London, the Smithfield inns catered for the northern

c

traffic, while Holborn received travellers and vehicles from the West, and Bishopsgate those from East Anglia. The inns of Southwark accommodated the south-borne traffic, and these, if another claim to fame were needed, could boast to have been the forcing-houses of perhaps the greatest school of drama that the world has known, for many of the earlier Elizabethan plays were produced in their yards. But it was not only such great inn-yards that were used for stage performances; itinerant bands of players roamed the countryside, their humble properties stacked in little carts, and gave performances in alehouse tap-rooms, barns, and even the great kitchens of farm-houses. The medieval mystery plays were at first still the favourites, but, as the century proceeded, these gave way to enactments of popular legends, garbled stories from the classics, and extemporised allegories. Shakespeare's Bottoms, Snugs, Quinces, and Flutes had their prototypes in real life all over the country.

A fine range of Elizabethan inns still exists along the main roads leading out of London, notably on the way to Ipswich, though these have not infrequently been disguised behind later frontages. It is impossible to write in any detail of all the fine houses that remain from this intriguing period (a number are described in fuller detail in the next two chapters), but mention should certainly be made of the magnificent *Feathers* at Ludlow (8), with its richly moulded plaster ceilings; the great inns of Chester, *The Falcon* (p. 44) and *The Bear and Billet* (66); the stone-built *Peacock* at Rowsley (13); *The Reindeer* at Banbury, which has the date 1570 over its gateway and contained the famous panelled Globe Room, added in 1637 and now in America; *The Rose and Crown* at Sudbury in Suffolk, formerly *The Black Horse*, where Gainsborough was born; *The Red Lion* at Colchester (16); *The Ostrich* at Colnbrook; and many others. All provided a full and wholesome fare for the traveller, which reflected the changes in the national diet that had gradually taken place since the Reformation. Now a good Protestant would no longer eat fish, which had formerly been in great demand, but coarse meats, fresh or salted, were

7 THE NEW INN, GLOUCESTER. A corner of the famous
galleried courtyard

8 THE FEATHERS, LUDLOW, SHROPSHIRE. This famous Elizabethan inn is one of the sights of the lovely little market-town on the Welsh Border

consumed in huge quantities, with slabs of bread made from a meal that was often anything but pure. Strong ale generally washed down a meal, but foreign wines were growing increasingly popular. These were usually heady decoctions from Spain and Italy, with French wines such

THE 'OSTRICH,' COLNBROOK, AN OLD COACHING INN
ON THE BATH ROAD

as Gascon and Guyon, and sweet drinks like sack and Malmsey. It was the adolescence of the Renaissance spirit in this country, and, as happens in adolescence, the drinkers often found it hard to realise when they had had enough, and evenings spent at the tavern were liable to end in brawls or even fierce fights. The young Marlowe, whose genius might even have rivalled that of Shakespeare, was killed in such a tavern brawl, and, according to a picturesque contemporary testimony, "died swearing."

On the close and intimate connections existing at this time between the taverns and literary circles in London, much could be written. Ben Jonson, as is well known, had a wide first-hand knowledge of the London inns; and his slighting reference in *Bartholomew Fair* to the dull wits of the day as "Three Cranes, Mitre and Mermaid men" is quoted *in extenso* on another page (46). *The Three Cranes* was near the river and the present Thames Street, not far from London Bridge, and it was at *The Mermaid* in Bread Street that Sir Walter Raleigh founded his famous literary circle, which knew Shakespeare, Webster, and a crowd of the Elizabethan poets. The skirmish of wits at such gatherings is neatly sketched in a verse letter from Beaumont to Jonson, who often alluded to the place:—

> At Bread Street's Mermaid having dined and merry,
> Proposed to go to Holborn in a wherry.

But this would hardly have been the ideal after-dinner trip, from all accounts, along the noisome Fleet River, which was used as a convenient chute for the City's garbage. The poet's favourite haunt, however, was *The Devil*, in Fleet Street, near his lodging over a comb-makers, once *The Devil and St. Dunstan*, with a sign showing the Saint gripping the Evil One by the nose with his red-hot pincers. In spite of slighting references to its wine, he drew up its twenty-four extremely 'Convivial Rules,' which are still preserved at Child's Bank, which was erected on the site in 1788. The inn continued to be the resort of writers and poets for two centuries, and is referred to by Pepys, Swift, and Addison.

*   *   *

There is a good deal of interesting data available for the student of inns and road travel in the seventeenth century. In spite of spasmodic attempts at legislation, the difficulties attending the traveller were still great, and in

9   THE LYGON ARMS, BROADWAY, WORCESTERSHIRE.   The famous inn of the famous village at the foot
of the Cotswolds

10 THE DOLPHIN, HIGHAM, NORFOLK. This fine Elizabethan building on the outskirts of Norwich was once used as the Bishop's Palace

11 THE TROUT, GODSTOW, OXFORDSHIRE. Known to generations of Thames fishermen and Oxford undergraduates

12 THE SONDES ARMS, ROCKINGHAM, NORTHAMPTONSHIRE, in its stone-built Midland village

13 THE PEACOCK, ROWSLEY, DERBYSHIRE. A fine Elizabethan inn near Haddon Hall

14 THE WHITE HART, SCOLE, NORFOLK. This splendid coaching inn was built by a Norwich merchant, James Peck, in 1655, but has lost its famous sign spanning the roadway, which was one of the wonders of the district

winter many of the roads were practically impassable either for horses or waggons. It is recorded that in the Weald of Kent it was customary in the autumn to plough them up, and lay the top soil in a half-circle to dry. That the surfaces at all seasons were villainous is hardly surprising, since famers still employed oxen to drag their waggons, and used heavy sledges to transport timber. In some parts of the country they ploughed right across the highway, while not the slightest attention was ever given to the repair of by-roads. Generally speaking, the seventeenth-century road lacked contour, drainage, direction-posts, milestones, or often any indication that it was intended as a road at all beyond the deep wheel-ruts that seared its mud. Waggons were simply hauled along by main force; and as late as the Restoration, Ralph Thoresby, the antiquary, found considerable difficulty in tracing his way along the Great North Road between Barnby Moor and Tuxford, and actually lost it altogether between Doncaster and York.

For much of our knowledge of the inns and road life during the first half of the seventeenth century we must be grateful to that extraordinary being, John Taylor, 'Poeta Aquaticus,' waterman, wanderer, innkeeper, Royalist, controversialist, and pamphleteer. If, from the literary aspect, his varied and voluminous output is often negligible, he certainly made the most of his small gifts for facile versifying and picturesque scurrility, and the accounts of his journeys still make amusing reading. One of his achievements was to prepare a list of the taverns within thirty miles of London, some 686 in all, and his *Carriers' Cosmographie* of 1637 is an interesting summary of communications between London and places in the Home Counties before the days of stage coaches, indicating a crowd of inns that served as forwarding depots for a vast and ramifying carriers' service. The lists of these inns show that while the public-house is one of the most enduring features in English social history, the changes to which it has been subjected over a period of some three centuries are thorough and far-reaching, to say the least of it. Taylor's journeys, which were the stock-in-trade of his curious profession, ranged from Scotland to Wales and Cornwall, and as a traveller he was only rivalled by the redoubtable Mrs. Celia Fiennes, who, however, must be credited with braving the horrors of execrable roads and villainous accommodation for the sheer fun of the thing. Taylor's publicity methods, including the issue of a preliminary prospectus and the canvassing of potential subscribers to the book of the journey before it was begun, would command the reverent appreciation of a modern advertising expert or professional globe-trotter. On his *Penyles Pilgrimage* to Edinburgh, to be carried out without spending a penny or asking for any assistance on the way, he took care to have his advent well announced, with an appeal to the sporting instincts of the innkeeping community which usually resulted in an uproarious welcome, and the freedom of the house. His usual reception thus formed the utter antithesis to that afforded the wandering German pastor, C. P. Moritz, about a century and a half later, who, as a pedestrian, encountered the considerable snobbery of the innkeeping class, spiced with the innate national prejudice of the period against foreigners of every kind (see pp. 82, 83). Taylor had a way of his own when it came to retaliation, and being dissatisfied with his treatment by a Daventry landlady, made elegant reference in print to the "warte on her snowte," and advised travellers generally "to balke that inn." On his Scottish tour, he actually penetrated to Braemar, where he enjoyed a hunting expedition with the Earl of Mar; and Ben Jonson, who was on his own pedestrian pilgrimage to Hawthornden, gave his competitor, at Leith, a piece of gold in which to drink his health in England.

If travel was on the increase during the period of the Commonwealth, the innkeeper was subjected to the pressure of restrictions more severe than even the irritating pettiness of present-day interference. In his *History of Hitchin*, Mr. Hine quotes the following, as promulgated in 1656:—

Foreasmuch as His Highness the Lord Protector of the Commonwealth hath taken special note of the mischiefs and

15   THE TALBOT, OUNDLE, NORTHAMPTONSHIRE.   A fine Elizabethan inn of
     Cotswold stone in its little Midland town

16   THE RED LION, COLCHESTER.   Several centuries have left their
mark on this graceful old frontage

17   THE KING'S HEAD, SHREWSBURY.   A fine old house dating from
the reign of Henry VII, whose sign hangs outside it

great disorders which daily happen and are committed in Taverns, Innes and Alehouses . . . the Justices of this County of Hertford are enjoined to take special care for the effectual suppressing of all such alehouse keepers as are, or shall be, convicted of the prophanation of the Lord's Day by receiving into their houses any company, or of swearing, drunkenness, suffering tippling, gaming, or playing at Tables, Billiard Table, Shovel-Board, Cards, Dice, Ninepins, Pigeon-holes, Trunks, or of keeping Bowling Alley or Bowling Green or any of them, or of any other games.

*   *   *

At the close of the Civil War, a stage coach service had been for the first time established on some of the trunk roads leading out of London. Coaches were run to Winchester, York, and Newcastle, and in 1657 a service was advertised to Chester three days a week, a journey that took four days and cost thirty-five shillings. These early enterprises were followed by others, for example, services to Preston, Lancaster, and Kendal, and to Exeter and Plymouth. In spite of the discomfort of the ill-sprung lumbering vehicles, and the manifold dangers of a countryside overrun with undesirables and vagrants of every kind, from the romantic highwayman, with his velvet mask and Mechlin ruffles (probably a Royalist soldier-of-fortune out of a job), to the common sneak-thief of the inn-yard, or cut-purse loitering in a roadside thicket, the new services were patronised and prospered. The great revolution in road travel had begun.

Naturally in such a revolution the inns played a prominent part. The large houses flourished on the influx of new custom, and on their new-found importance as stages in a regular coaching system; and the amenities they offered must have been a considerable comfort to the shaken passenger deposited there after an arduous day's journeying. The rigours of this early coach travel, somewhat magnified for propaganda purposes, were entertainingly set down by one John Cresset in a pamphlet published about 1672, which is worth quoting *in extenso:*—

What advantage is it to Man's health, to be called out of their Beds into these Coaches an hour before day in the morning, to be hurried in them from place to place, till one hour, two, or three within night; insomuch that, after sitting all day in the summertime stifled with heat, and choaked with dust; or the Wintertime, starving and freezing with cold, or choaked with filthy Fogs, they are often brought into their Inns by Torchlight, when it is too late to sit up and get a Supper; and next morning they are forced into the coach so early, that they can get no Breakfast? What addition is this to Mens Health or Business, to ride all day with strangers, oftentimes sick, ancient, diseased Persons, or young Children crying, to whose humours they are obliged to be subject . . . and many times crippled by the crowd of the Boxes and Bundles? Is it for a Man's Health to travel with tired Jades, to be laid fast in the foul Wayes, and forced to wade up to the Knees in mire; afterwards to sit in the cold, till Teams of Horses can be sent to pull the Coach out? Is it for their Health to travel in rotten Coaches, and to have their Tackle, or Perch, or Axletree broken, and then to wait three or four hours (sometimes half a day) to have them mended again, and then to travel all night to make good their Stage? Is it to a Man's pleasure, or advantagious to their Healths and Business, to travel with a mixt Company that he knows not how to converse with; to be affronted by the rudeness of a surly, dogged, cussing, illnatured Coachman; necessitated to Lodge, or Bait, at the worst Inns on the Road, where there is no accomodation fit for Gentlemen; and this merely because the Owners of the Inns, and the Coachman, are agreed together to cheat the Guests? . . . Is it for advantage of a Man's Business, that though he have a concern of great weight or moment to transact upon the Road as he goes along, yet if it live but a stones cast out of the Coach-way the Coachman will not drive thither, nor stay for him at any place, except the Baiting or Lodging-Houses where he calls, where they change horses; and there stay no longer than he pleases neither. To be forced, whatever accident, or sickness or illness happens, to ride these Coachmans Stages, though never so late in the night, or else to be left in the middle of a Journey in a strange place? . . . Yet this hath been many Persons of good Qualities case; though they have offered to pay the whole Coach-hire, and all the Passengers charges, and to have put into an Inn; yet have been denied, forced to ride, though in peril of their life, till midnight. And it is not hard to instance in many that have lost their lives by such usage.

Cresset was out to break the threatened monopoly of coach-borne traffic, and spared no pains to gather firsthand information on the inconveniences of coaching at

great disorders which daily happen and are committed in
Taverns, Innes and Alehouses . . . the Justices of this County
of Hertford are enjoined to take special care for the effectual
suppressing of all such alehouse keepers as are, or shall be,
convicted of the prophanation of the Lord's Day by receiving
into their houses any company, or of swearing, drunkenness,
suffering tippling, gaming, or playing at Tables, Billiard
Table, Shovel-Board, Cards, Dice, Ninepins, Pigeon-holes,
Trunks, or of keeping Bowling Alley or Bowling Green or
any of them, or of any other games.

*   *   *

At the close of the Civil War, a stage coach service had
been for the first time established on some of the trunk
roads leading out of London. Coaches were run to
Winchester, York, and Newcastle, and in 1657 a service
was advertised to Chester three days a week, a journey
that took four days and cost thirty-five shillings. These
early enterprises were followed by others, for example,
services to Preston, Lancaster, and Kendal, and to
Exeter and Plymouth. In spite of the discomfort of the
ill-sprung lumbering vehicles, and the manifold dangers
of a countryside overrun with undesirables and vagrants
of every kind, from the romantic highwayman, with his
velvet mask and Mechlin ruffles (probably a Royalist
soldier-of-fortune out of a job), to the common sneak-
thief of the inn-yard, or cut-purse loitering in a roadside
thicket, the new services were patronised and prospered.
The great revolution in road travel had begun.

Naturally in such a revolution the inns played a prominent part. The large houses flourished on the influx of
new custom, and on their new-found importance as stages
in a regular coaching system; and the amenities they
offered must have been a considerable comfort to the
shaken passenger deposited there after an arduous day's
journeying. The rigours of this early coach travel, somewhat magnified for propaganda purposes, were entertainingly set down by one John Cresset in a pamphlet
published about 1672, which is worth quoting *in
extenso*:—

What advantage is it to Man's health, to be called out of their
Beds into these Coaches an hour before day in the morning,

to be hurried in them from place to place, till one hour, two, or three within night; insomuch that, after sitting all day in the summertime stifled with heat, and choaked with dust; or the Wintertime, starving and freezing with cold, or choaked with filthy Fogs, they are often brought into their Inns by Torchlight, when it is too late to sit up and get a Supper; and next morning they are forced into the coach so early, that they can get no Breakfast? What addition is this to Mens Health or Business, to ride all day with strangers, oftentimes sick, ancient, diseased Persons, or young Children crying, to whose humours they are obliged to be subject . . . and many times crippled by the crowd of the Boxes and Bundles? Is it for a Man's Health to travel with tired Jades, to be laid fast in the foul Wayes, and forced to wade up to the Knees in mire; afterwards to sit in the cold, till Teams of Horses can be sent to pull the Coach out? Is it for their Health to travel in rotten Coaches, and to have their Tackle, or Perch, or Axletree broken, and then to wait three or four hours (sometimes half a day) to have them mended again, and then to travel all night to make good their Stage? Is it to a Man's pleasure, or advantagious to their Healths and Business, to travel with a mixt Company that he knows not how to converse with; to be affronted by the rudeness of a surly, dogged, cussing, illnatured Coachman; necessitated to Lodge, or Bait, at the worst Inns on the Road, where there is no accomodation fit for Gentlemen; and this merely because the Owners of the Inns, and the Coachman, are agreed together to cheat the Guests? . . . Is it for advantage of a Man's Business, that though he have a concern of great weight or moment to transact upon the Road as he goes along, yet if it live but a stones cast out of the Coach-way the Coachman will not drive thither, nor stay for him at any place, except the Baiting or Lodging-Houses where he calls, where they change horses; and there stay no longer than he pleases neither. To be forced, whatever accident, or sickness or illness happens, to ride these Coachmans Stages, though never so late in the night, or else to be left in the middle of a Journey in a strange place? . . . Yet this hath been many Persons of good Qualities case; though they have offered to pay the whole Coach-hire, and all the Passengers charges, and to have put into an Inn; yet have been denied, forced to ride, though in peril of their life, till midnight. And it is not hard to instance in many that have lost their lives by such usage.

Cresset was out to break the threatened monopoly of coach-borne traffic, and spared no pains to gather firsthand information on the inconveniences of coaching at

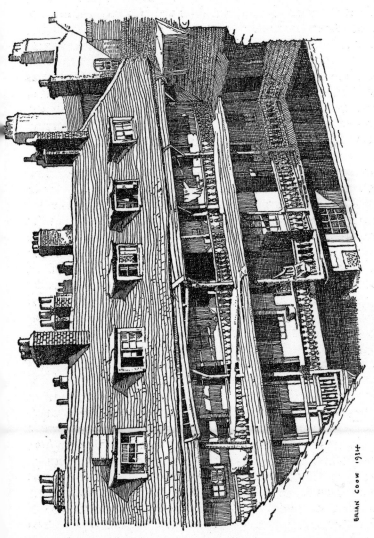

THE OLD 'OXFORD ARMS' IN WARWICK LANE, LONDON, AS IT EXISTED
SIXTY YEARS AGO

BRIAN COOK 1934

D

this period. But the new system of 'rapid' travelling had come to stay, and, by the close of the century, the practice of innkeeping had reached a very much higher level of efficiency than Cresset would have had his public suppose. From the mass of contemporary evidence available, it would seem that landlords were now genuinely eager to do their best for travellers. The rooms were well furnished at the larger inns, which catered for regular as well as for chance custom, the supply of food and drink was generous, the stables were roomy, and the ostlers, waiters, and serving-maids generally civil and obliging. It is a fascinating occupation to reconstruct the appearance of one of the larger coaching inns at the close of the seventeenth century, such as *The Stamford Hotel*, now rebuilt (33), as it must have appeared in the old 'York and London' days. Perhaps as many as sixty travellers would be entertained there at the same time, and in the yard would be a number of the new private leather coaches, one or two public stages, and a huge York to London stage waggon. The stables would be full of horses, some just in and still steaming, others smartly groomed and ready to start out again. The ostlers would be noisily at their tasks, while the coachmen and wag-goners forgathered at the tap. The host would be every-where at once, at one moment bowing in new arrivals, at another superintending the delivery of fodder, and later snatching a moment to drink a glass with an old acquaintance. It was Sir Thomas Overbury who described a landlord as "a mixture of double beer and fellowship."

The inn buildings of the seventeenth century cover a wide range of architectural development. In *The Dolphin*, just outside Norwich (10), for instance, which, though parts of it are earlier, bears the date of 1615, and was once used as the Bishop's Palace, we find a remarkable survival of Tudor methods in a building constructed of the characteristic East-Anglian flint. Other typical inns of about the same period, illustrated in these pages, are *The Bell* at Stilton (3), a fine stone building of Cotswold type, *The Lygon Arms* at Broadway (9), and the stately gabled *Talbot* at Oundle (15). The beautiful *Haycock* at

19   THE GREYHOUND, CORFE, DORSET.   In the
shadow of the Castle knoll

18   BISLEY, GLOUCESTERSHIRE.   A small
village inn in the South Cotswolds

21 THE GEORGE, BUCKDEN, HUNTINGDONSHIRE.
A famous Georgian coaching inn on the
Great North Road

20 THE DUKE'S HEAD, KING'S LYNN, NORFOLK.
Built *circa* 1680 as a mansion by the talented
local architect, Henry Bell

Wansford (25), formerly on, now by-passed by, the Great
North Road, and long a private house, is one of the
largest stone-built inns of the century, and reveals the
Cotswold tradition extending as far eastward as the
oolitic undulations of Huntingdonshire. *The White Hart*
at Scole (14), from which the famous sign (p. 61), extending like a triumphal archway across the road, has now
vanished, is delightfully characteristic of the mid seventeenth century in its ranges of stepped gables and tall
moulded brick chimneys; and of the Restoration are the
aristocratic little *Pomfret Arms* at Towcester (23), formerly
The Saracen's Head, immortalised in *Pickwick* as the
meeting-place of Slurk and Pott, *The Sea-Horse* at Deene,
The Greyhound at Corfe (19), and the present Judge's
Lodging, formerly part of the fine Georgian *Antelope* at
Dorchester.

The eighteenth century saw a tremendous increase in
the volume of wheeled traffic. Though, for the first half
of it at least, the state of the roads showed hardly any
improvement on the last century, the passing of the
Turnpike Act in 1755, which netted England with toll-
gates, inaugurated a comprehensive programme of repairs,
while the magnificent bridges of this period, that can still
be seen all over the country, testify to the improved
amenities of travel. At the same time, a great advance
was made in the design of the vehicles themselves, which
is very evident if we compare the stage-coach of
George I's reign with that in use at the close of the
century. In every type of vehicle, including the four-
wheeled farm cart, a lightening in design and construction
was observable, with the exception only of the stage-
waggons. These 'merchant-ships of the road' had changed
little in their massive, clumsy construction, though their
wheels were now made much broader in compliance
with an act of Parliament, in order to flatten out the ruts.
The body was built on heavy beams, and the 'tilt,' which
sheltered passengers and goods, followed the medieval
tradition. A great lanthorn slung in the forepart of this
tilt warned travellers by gig or chaise of the oncoming
danger.

By the year 1750 there were innumerable waggons of this type on the roads, as well as smaller carts used for conveying coal, timber, and iron. Though these naturally somewhat impeded the faster traffic, the speed of the stage-coach from London to York had been increased from the five miles an hour of 1720 to a round average of seven; and in 1754 the 'flying coach' from Manchester to London was only four and a half days on the road. In 1768 the charge for coach travelling was a shilling for five miles, and the majority of coaches made between fifty and sixty miles a day, though on level journeys sometimes seventy, eighty, or even a hundred miles were accomplished, as to Southampton or Norwich. In 1775 coaches were running with eight passengers inside and ten on the roof. The *Annual Register* of that year informs us that the number of public coaches, flys, machines, and diligences on the roads exceeded 400, while the total number of four-wheeled carriages was some 17,000. Moreover, for those who could afford it, the posting system now provided a means of transit at a hitherto unprecedented speed. With frequent changes of horse, these smart new post-chaises could cover the ground at a spanking pace, whirling clouds of dust over the hedgerows in summer, and plastering their postilion-drivers to the neck in mud during the winter: paying toll outside Bath one morning, rattling, swaying, creaking through the countryside all day, and drawing up in Berkeley Square before nightfall.

So vast an increase in traffic inevitably reacted on the inns, as much from the point of view of architectural design as of comfort and internal economy. The majority of houses built at this time in the country towns and larger villages, together with those of earlier date reclothed in a classical coat of brick or stone, have a pleasing family resemblance in the design of their features, though the spacing and proportions of their trim, white-sashed windows were chiefly relied upon for the harmony of the general effect. The *White Horse* at Haslemere (115) and *The Georges* at Buckden (21), West Wycombe (37), and Axminster, are charmingly typical of the first half of

23 THE POMFRET ARMS, TOWCESTER, NORTHAMPTON-
SHIRE. Formerly *The Saracen's Head*, this beautiful
Restoration house is commended in *Pickwick*

22 THE KING'S ARMS, DORCHESTER, DORSET.
A convivially pot-bellied Regency front

24 THE WHITE HORSE, EATON SOCON, BEDFORDSHIRE.
A pleasant Georgian frontage on the Great North Road

25 THE HAYCOCK, WANSFORD, NORTHAMPTONSHIRE. Long a private
house, this beautiful seventeenth-century inn has now reverted to its
old calling, though by-passed by the Great North Road

26 THE SIR JOHN FALSTAFF, GAD'S HILL, KENT. The site of
Sir John's carousings with Prince Hal in *Henry IV*

27 THE ANCHOR, LIPHOOK, HAMPSHIRE. A great coaching house
with a nautical air on the Portsmouth Road

28 THE SWAN, DENHAM, BUCKINGHAMSHIRE. A pleasant little Georgian inn in its quiet village street

the eighteenth century, still generally built with the low
entrance archway common before coaches began to carry
outside passengers. After the accession of George III,

AN ELEGANT SMALLER INN OF THE EARLY GEORGIAN PERIOD, THE
'KING'S HEAD AND BELL' AT ABINGDON

when outside travelling became general, these archways
were often heightened by the landlords to accommodate
the taller coaches. In the sturdy fashion of the time, out-

side passengers were now often treated as a superior race
of Spartans, in another category to the anaemic spinsters
and querulous invalids who occupied the dark, stuffy
recesses of the interior, with its heavy redolence of
leather.

The tired traveller, arriving at one of the large solid
inns of the later eighteenth century, would generally have
been justified in expecting the highest degree of "comfort
and elegance." If the coach was timed to stop for half an
hour to change horses and enable the passengers to dine,
the waiters would be standing at the door in readiness to
assist him with his hat, shawl, and coat. The landlord and
landlady would be waiting in the hall, where there would
be a good display of cold meats, game pies, cheeses, and
pastries on view in a special glazed cupboard. The
coffee-room or dining parlour would reveal an immense
central table, round or rectangular, laid in readiness for
the meal, with good plated cutlery and spotless table-
linen. Some inns could boast a special dining-room for
coach passengers, while the upstairs bedrooms, each with
its curtained four-poster and good plain furniture, often
of mahogany, including a mirror, a washing-table, and a
wig-stand, were still generally known by individual names
such as the Moon, Star, Crescent, or Paragon.

Nevertheless, as was after all inevitable in such a
personal profession as innkeeping, there was a good deal
of variation in the standard of hospitality offered, as
contemporary documents reveal. The Dean of Exeter
writes to a friend in 1767 that he "cannot commend the
inns at Plymouth, they are like those in other seaports,
neither very neat nor quiet." Arthur Young, in the list
of inns he made on his *Southern Tour*, wrote down six of
the thirty-seven as "very bad and very dear," *The Bush*
at Wanstead being "dirty and impertinent," and *The
George* at Winchester "dirty and dear, but civil." Pastor
Moritz, leaving his inn at Windsor after a very painful
stay, was coolly asked by the waiter for a tip. "I gave
him three-halfpence," recorded the indefatigable divine,
"on which he saluted me with the heartiest 'God d——n
you, Sir!' I have ever heard. At the door stood the cross

29 THE BRIDGE HOTEL, NEWHAVEN, SUSSEX. Where Louis Philippe
began his exile

30 THE HOP POLE, TEWKESBURY, GLOUCESTERSHIRE.
Where Mr Pickwick stopped to dine

maid, who also accosted me with 'pray remember the chamber-maid!' 'Yes, yes,' said I, 'I shall long remember your most ill-mannered behaviour, and shameful incivility'; and so I gave her nothing."

But such treatment was the exception rather than the rule, and it was generally impossible for an inn to thrive long on bad management and rudeness to travellers. An Irish Gentleman, on a *Journey Through England*, in 1752, paid only 6d. at Liverpool for "a very good supper, consisting of veal cutlets, pigeons, asparagus, lamb and salad, apple-pie and tarts." The great terminal inns of later Georgian times were on the whole thoroughly well organised to meet every requirement of their clients, including such refinements as the use of a warming-pan before the guest retired to take the chill off clean sheets; and the extent of some of them is probably not sufficiently realised, such as *The George and Blue Boar* in Holborn (*v.* p. 58), the starting-place of the Glasgow coach, which could boast 40 bedrooms, stabling for 52 horses, 7 coach-houses, and a dry drive seventy yards long.

At the close of the century and during the early years of the next, when coaching was all the fashion, and men of quality aped the dress and language of stage-coachmen, and drove their own four-in-hands along the highways, the great Regency illustrators, such as Rowlandson, Pollard, and the Alkens, loved to depict the life of the inns and roads in all its bustle and cheerful vigour. Their drawings and prints show us the gaily painted and polished coaches borne out of the inn yards at a smart trot by high-stepping blacks, greys, and piebalds, the coachman flicking his whip and the guard sounding a vigorous fanfare on his horn at the little knot of ostlers and spectators which assembles daily at the same time to watch the cheerful and familiar scene. We can witness the arrival of a private coach party at an inn, the landlord bowing an obsequious welcome to the stout turbanned lady, with her lapdogs and companion, the ostler exchanging a wink with the chambermaid as they follow the procession upstairs to the Paragon, weighed down with all sorts of preposterous baggage. Or we can attend a hunt

breakfast in the private parlour of an inn, and see the
local gentry taking its ease in a room littered with wine-
coolers and bottles, sprawling with wigs awry in every
attitude of slight or advanced intoxication, while the
pink-coated master gives the toast, a cup in one hand
and a dead fox's brush in the other.

The Regency saw the culmination of the inns'
prosperity. With the building of the railways, the
importance and dignity of the great old houses began to
decline, while in the bigger towns they were often
replaced by large and unlovely hotels of a new type, a
subject which is treated in more detail in the next
chapter. The reign of Queen Victoria saw a long eclipse
of the great tradition of innkeeping in this country, and
wherever the germ of the new industrialism developed,
the old houses were generally replaced by the reeking,
flaring gin-palaces of the nineteenth century, often
provided by the local brewers as their idea of a seemly
and appropriate background for democratic leisure. But
these again for the most part belong to the past, and the
brewing fraternity, though it can seldom altogether
resist the allure of oak beams, a rough-cast finish, and an
old-world air, is nowadays generally doing its best to
provide decent hygienic places of refreshment, where food
and drink can be obtained at reasonable prices. And along
the great highways, which despite the modern arterial
roads and by-passes are still largely the same roads that
have been used through the centuries, the old inns are
coming to life again after their long decline. The development of the motor has brought new life to their yards, a
clatter of plates to their coffee-rooms, and the old familiar
hum of conversation around their taps, whether they now
be called lounges, smoking-rooms, or American Bars.
The inns, in fact, have been given a new lease of life and a
new opportunity. Let the proprietors rise to it with energy
and vision, take the same scrupulous pride in the historic
houses in their charge as did the innkeepers of old, and
thus help in a revival of the true and grand tradition of
real English hospitality.

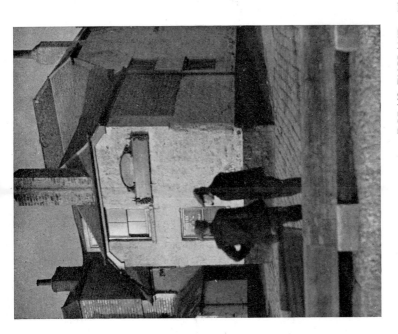

31, 32   DORA'S ENGLAND.   The afternoon vigil before opening time

33 THE STAMFORD HOTEL, STAMFORD, LINCOLNSHIRE. A Regency
inn on modern hotel lines. The distinguished classical front was designed
circa 1820 by John Linnell Bond

II

THE LARGER INN

From a general survey it is a long trail to the particular. A detailed list of old inns appears at the end of this volume. A few large inns are in this chapter treated in detail, not because others, illustrated in the plates or mentioned in the list at the end, are unworthy of such treatment, but because they will give the student of inns a chance of studying a group of fine and characteristic houses in a leisurely way. There is obviously not room to treat of them all.

We have therefore selected a few of the larger inns, arranged them in chronological order, and described them, as expressive of the period, or variety of periods, to which they belong.

At one time the whole of the manor of Norton St. Philip, including *The George Inn* (34), belonged to the Carthusian Priory of Hinton, and this seems to explain the fact that the inn also did service as a market, for in the reign of Edward I both the weekly market and the annual wool fair were held under the Priory auspices. In those days the large upper room was used by the traders in wool, which formed the chief industry of Norton St. Philip, while the rest of the building did a roaring business as a hostelry. When first built early in the fifteenth century, the whole structure was of stone. The projecting half-timber storeys, which divide the front horizontally into three divisions, are of later date, as the stone quoins at the gable-ends show. This alteration was a result of the destruction by fire of the upper part of the inn in the late fifteenth or early sixteenth century, when opportunity was taken to patch and alter the ancient house to its present form. The earlier stone porch and the bay windows are practically as first built, and even the back exhibits some unusually picturesque features. For example, the octagonal stone turret-stairway, and a fragment of the ancient gallery, indicate something

THE MEDIEVAL BACK OF 'THE GEORGE,' NORTON ST. PHILIP,
SHOWING THE TURRET STAIRCASE

of the original arrangement in this quarter, and here also
much old stonework remains, with the original traceried
windows. It is for the most part as genuine a survival

34   THE GEORGE, NORTON ST PHILIP, SOMERSET.   A great medieval "Wool Inn," with memories of Monmouth's rising

35 THE OLD GEORGE, SALISBURY. Where Pepys 'slept in a silk bed'

of an early inn as any chronicler could wish for; its very stones are eloquent of the social life of the Middle Ages. And to pass to a later period, here Cromwell was lodged with a party of his Roundheads during the Civil War, while, not many years after, an attempt was made on the life of the handsome Monmouth as he stood at one of its windows.

The Pilgrims' Inn at Glastonbury (4), built between 1470 and 1475 by Abbot John de Selwood for accommodating pilgrims and others visiting the abbey, is expressive of the period when the Church still exercised a dominant influence on social life. The inn, The George Hotel as it is now called, faces south, and the fine free-stone of which it is built has stood the test of time and weather unimpaired. The front is only 34 feet wide, but the building looks twice the size. The original designer knew his business well, for he contrived to embody in one design, without any sense of overcrowding, the dissimilar features of a three-storeyed bay, a large arch-way, a projecting bracket for the sign, and a number of buttresses. The result is one of the finest surviving examples of a contemporary design in panelled stone-work, at this period such a distinctive feature of the town buildings of the West Country. The majority of the panels are pierced and glazed, the remainder, not required for windows, being filled in with solid masonry. Of the three carved panels over the entrance archway, two display the armorial bearings of the abbey and Edward IV respectively, while the third is a shield left plain without arms. Beside the arch is the stone pier which carries the bracket supporting the sign, originally St. George and the Dragon, carved and painted in gay colours. The little shields in the cornices are carved with crosses, and the interlaced initials of the patron-builder, 'I. S.,' occur on one side. From between the battlements of the bay-window a carved figure looks out, holding a cup, the only one surviving of a series that testified to the medieval love of a simple joke, this time at the expense of the drinkers inside. Generally this inn is rich to look upon from without, and there can be little doubt

'THE GEORGE,' GLASTONBURY, FORMERLY 'THE PILGRIMS' INN'

that at one time its inner fittings, of which no trace now
exists, were of a quality far beyond the ordinary, befitting
the dignity of the abbey establishment.

Another large inn of Tudor times, *The King's Head* at Aylesbury, is a timber-frame structure that exhibits in the workmanship of its great window of twenty lights (p. 28), as in the moulded ribs of its external and internal framings, that leisurely extravagance in time, labour, and material that is characteristic of the medieval builders. The traceried timber window at the back of *The Luttrell Arms*, Dunster (p. 29), is of equally fine craftsmanship, in curious contrast to the austerity of the stone front of the house (107). The remains of the great timber inns at St. Albans, as in French Row and the old wing of *The White Hart*, show once again the inns of the cathedral cities and abbey towns to have been buildings of the first rank. In York, many ancient inns have vanished, but the houses in such streets as The Shambles, with their projecting upper storeys almost meeting across the road, nodding gables and massive timberings, still present the finest survival of the 'scenery' of town life during the Middle Ages. While in London no great medieval inns survive, there are many built on the same sites as their medieval ancestors. And London remains obstinately a confederation of villages, with Westminster still another world from Southwark or Whitechapel, and in the centre of all, the City, a medieval-planned town complete in itself. Here at least is a confusion medieval enough for the most retrograde; and since the old inn buildings have vanished, we must content ourselves with their sites, which often evoke memories of extraordinary fascination and interest.

The Tabard, selected by Chaucer as the starting-place of his Canterbury Pilgrims, was the most famous of the great inns of Southwark, which absorbed most of the London-bound traffic from South-East England.

> Byfel that in that sesoun on a day
> In Southwark at the Tabard as I lay . . .

So begins the famous *Tales*. Chaucer gives the name of the landlord, Henry Bailly, who represented Southwark in the Parliament held at Westminster in 1376. Another

THE GREAT TUDOR WINDOW, IN WOOD, OF TWENTY LIGHTS, AT
'THE KING'S HEAD,' AYLESBURY

36 THE GEORGE, SOUTHWARK, LONDON. A galleried fragment of
the last of the great coaching inns of the Borough

37 THE GEORGE, WEST WYCOMBE, BUCKINGHAMSHIRE.
The Georgian inn of the village preserved for the Nation

CARVED WOODWORK WINDOWS AT THE BACK OF 'THE
LUTTRELL ARMS,' DUNSTER

great Southwark inn was *The White Hart*, probably built
in the fourteenth century, its sign being derived from
the badge of Richard II. Jack Cade made it his head-

quarters during the insurrection of 1450. In 1529 the
inn was still flourishing, for there is a letter in existence
asking for an appointment there with Thomas Cromwell.
In 1669 the back quarters were destroyed by fire. What
is left of *The George Inn* (36) stands between the sites of
The Tabard and *The White Hart*, and old records show
that this extraordinarily interesting galleried fragment
dates from the first quarter of the seventeenth century,
when the inn was rebuilt in brick and timber following
a fire. Fire was certainly the chief enemy of the Southwark inns, but we must be thankful that this portion of
one of them has been spared, in a quarter of rumbling
drays and large, shabby, Dickensian warehouses, to
remind us of the former spick-and-span importance of
this great traffic terminus of the old London.

Over the river, *The Bull* in Bishopsgate Street had
persistent associations with the eastern roads, and,
curiously enough, is still advertised at Ely as a place of
call for stage-waggons. It was here that Burbage and
his band of players obtained a patent from Queen
Elizabeth to erect a theatre; and it is recorded that
Anthony Bacon, the brother of the great Francis, lived
in his youth not far from it under the watchful eye of
his mother, who dreaded the baneful influence of the
plays and players on her impressionable son. On the east
side of Warwick Lane was another galleried inn, *The Bell*,
where Archbishop Leighton died in 1684, having re-
marked prophetically through his later years that "if he
were to choose a place to die in, it should be an Inn; it
looked like a pilgrim's going home, to whom this world
was all as an inn, and was weary of the noise and confusion in it." Sixty years ago the old *Oxford Arms* was
still standing in the same neighbourhood (p. 15), one of
the most interesting of the great inns of Central London,
approached by a passage from Warwick Lane. Bounded
on the west by London Wall, it spread to the south as
far as Amen Corner, with a glimpse of Old St. Paul's
from its busy yard. The house was rebuilt after the
Great Fire, and conformed to the galleried courtyard
type made familiar by *The George* at Southwark, though

38 THE COCK AND THE BULL, STONY STRATFORD, BUCKINGHAMSHIRE. The Georgian twins whose gossiping during the Napoleonic Wars proverbially gave rise to the expression "a cock and bull story"

39 THE BULL, ROCHESTER, KENT. The main coach entrance

40 THE BULL, ROCHESTER, KENT. The interior of the yard

it was designed on a much larger scale than the latter. An advertisement in the *London Gazette* for March 1672–3, reads: "These are to give notice that Edward Bartlett, Oxford carrier, hath removed his inn in London from The Swan at Holborn Bridge to The Oxford in Warwick Lane, where he did inn before the Fire, his coaches and waggons going forth on their usual days, Mondays, Wednesdays, and Fridays. He hath also a hearse, and all things convenient to carry a Corpse to

THE YARD OF THE OLD 'BULL AND MOUTH' IN ST. MARTIN'S-LE-GRAND
(AFTER T. H. SHEPHERD)

any part of England." At the time of Waterloo, the *Oxford Arms* was owned by Edward Sherman, who was also the proprietor of the vast and splendid *Bull and Mouth* in St. Martin's Lane, and one of the largest posting-masters in London. In 1868 some of the rooms were let as tenements, but the carriers' business survived, long-distance waggons and carts still setting out from there regularly for Oxford and other places on the western roads. In 1875 the old buildings were demolished.

In the days before steam, Charing Cross had its

F

coaching terminus in the famous Georgian *Golden Cross*,
a five-storeyed building of brick, with elegant sashed
shop-fronts on either side of the coach entrance. In the
heyday of its prosperity, long before Smirke rebuilt it
as an hotel, it was known affectionately among travellers
as 'The Bull and Mouth of the West,' and until late in
the eighteenth century it still had before it a signpost
and long water-trough, evidence of the old rural character
of the district, so near and yet so far from the City.
With the dawn of the nineteenth century, the most
important coaching terminus was *The White Horse Cellar*,
near the site of the present Berkeley Hotel in Piccadilly,
a favourite rendezvous of the more prosperous Lon-
doners, where on summer evenings crowds would gather
to watch the West Country mails departing. "The finest
sight in the Metropolis," Hazlitt wrote, "is the setting
off of the mail coaches from Piccadilly. The horses paw
the ground and are impatient to be gone, as if conscious
of the precious burden they convey. The mail carts
drive up, and the transfer of packages is made, and at a
given signal, off they start. . . . How we hate the Putney
and Brentford stages that draw up when they are gone!
Some persons think that the noblest object in Nature
is the ship launched on the bosom of the ocean; but
give me, for my private satisfaction, the mail coaches
that pour down Piccadilly of an evening, tear up the
pavement, and devour the way before them to the
Land's End."

In London, the stately eighteenth-century inn has
seldom survived, but in the provinces it dominates
many a High Street, where it sometimes rivals the Town
Hall or Market in architectural importance. On the
greater highways we likewise find the village inn
emulating something of the dignity of its town brother.
A typical country inn of this type is *The White Horse*
at Eaton Socon on the Great North Road (24). Here
is a house redolent of the atmosphere of Smollett's
tales; indeed, it may well be the identical one described
by the novelist in *Sir Lancelot Greaves*. Built originally
in the fifteenth century, it was pleasantly refronted about

41 THE GEORGE, STAMFORD, LINCOLNSHIRE. The famous coaching
inn, with a glimpse of the town and of St Mary's spire

42 THE WHITE HART, SALISBURY. An imposing example of 'county'
dignity in *circa* 1790

the middle of the eighteenth. At Pangbourne, *The George* was refaced with a three-storeyed façade with an amusing upper range of painted imitation 'windows,' as though some former proprietor had grown ashamed of the old Stuart building and wished to present a bolder front to his cramped attics. *The Cross Keys* at St. Neots underwent a transformation about the year 1730, when the front was newly bricked and the bay windows added; and much the same was done to the front of *The White Hart* at Ampthill in Bedfordshire, the author's 'local.' Nearer London, the three-storeyed *White Hart* at Southall, *The Lion* at Hartford Bridge, and *The Sir John Falstaff* at Gad's Hill (26), are all fine houses of early Georgian character. Fenny Stratford on Watling Street could once boast many inns, but to-day only the antiquary can trace them. There remain, however, *The Cock* and *The Bull* (38), two noted coaching inns, famous for the rumours that emanated from them during the eighteenth century concerning the Peninsular battles, traditionally giving rise to the cant expression 'a cock-and-bull story.'

Dr. Johnson knew *The Swan* at Lichfield, which has come down to us practically unaltered from the time when the great man was still being scolded by his mother. Another great inn of the mid-eighteenth century is *The Rutland Arms* at Newmarket, with its long racing associations, a classic essay in brick, with a pedimented feature over the courtyard gateway. *The Anchor* at Liphook (27) dates from about 1745, and *The Old George* at Aylesbury, now the headquarters of a territorial regiment, from about a quarter of a century later. Here until a few years ago most of the old plate was still in use, but lack of custom was the cause of its closing before the internal combustion engine gave new life to the roads. At Grantham are two remarkable examples of the third quarter of the eighteenth century in *The George* (46) and the new wing of *The Angel. The George* is an outstanding instance of the architectural taste of the day. It is a three-storeyed brick building with two pavilion features, terminating in a grouping of five windows. In the centre is a rusticated entry, with the

date 1789 on the keystone, but recent alterations have
deprived the inn of much of the character it possessed
when Nicholas Nickleby stopped outside it on his
journey to Dotheboys Hall. The additions to *The Angel*
rather resemble a block of chambers in the Middle
Temple, the courtyard fronts, no less than the extensive
stable ranges, presenting that trim, gentlemanly uni-
formity so characteristic of later eighteenth-century taste.
These sets of rooms were planned independently of the
medieval portion of the house, but a passage, lit by a
Palladian window, forms a bridge over the entrance
archway.

   One of the most agreeable Georgian inns is *The White
Horse* at Haslemere in Surrey (115). This house has the
unmistakable air of a rendezvous, if not of the nobility,
at least of the gentry. Jane Austen refers to *The Dolphin*
at Southampton, and so does Fanny Burney; and in our
own time it has been singled out as a favourite by
Mr. Belloc. *The Bull* at Royston, known affectionately to
generations of Cambridge undergraduates in the eighteenth and early nineteenth centuries, is still awaiting
rediscovery. *The Sugar Loaf* at Dunstable is another, but
larger, example of Georgian design, with *The Bull* at
Redbourne sharing the privilege of being a stopping-
place for the heavy coaches to the north-west, which
were horsed by Sherman. The Restoration front of *The
Rose and Crown* at Saffron Walden was remodelled in
1874 by Eden Nesfield, and is a rare example of a job
well done at this period by an architect who thoroughly
understood the character of the original building.

   At the same time it must be conceded that many
Georgian inns have little externally to recommend them
except their homeliness and simple dignity, though we
can often respect the modesty and reticence of their
designers, who generally understood the value of fine
proportions, and could dispose a range of sashed
windows, add a portico or shape an archway with the
best in London. Sometimes men of no mean talent were
employed, as must have been the case for *The Red Lion*
at Hatfield, which, standing just outside the town,

adjoining the park gates of the great house of the Cecils, has an air of dignified importance which, even at the lowest ebb of road travel, never quite deserted it. *The Swan Hotel* at Bedford is one of the most severe and correct of later eighteenth-century inns, having been built in 1794 from designs probably supplied by the architect of Carlton House, Henry Holland, who incorporated in it a seventeenth-century staircase from the dismantled mansion of Houghton Conquest. *The Swan* has all the refinements of a sober Whiggish country mansion of its period, and its atmosphere must have been a trifle frigid for the roaring heartiness of provincial beanfeasts during the Regency. Another house with genuine classical pretensions is *The White Hart* at Salisbury (42), which was rebuilt in its present form at the close of the eighteenth century to a three-storeyed design, with a striking Ionic portico feature; and if the windows have lost their trim white sashing, the life-size effigy of a white hart still surmounts the central pediment, and the great lamps on either side of the lower porch suggest, on a giant scale, those of the myriad coaches and carriages of its connection that have since passed for ever from the roads.

With the dawn of the nineteenth century, road travel became much more general among all grades of society; and if the nobility was still squeamish about using the public stage, the rising classes of professional men, manufacturers, small landowners, and the like, had no such scruples; so that the inns continued to thrive, even providing occasional hospitality for the great of the land, and Royalty. The eighteenth-century houses now often came to be regarded as out of date and old-fashioned, and, as the volume of traffic multiplied, existing inns were increasingly enlarged, refitted, or else entirely rebuilt, to conform with improved standards of comfort. And this comfort was on the whole very solid and real indeed. Probably at no time before or since have the English inns offered a finer hospitality than at the period of Waterloo. The sea-coal fires in the bedrooms, the abundant *table d'hôte* of good English fare, the prompt

and generally cheerful service, all compare badly with
the bleak beds, chipped ewers, and inedible five-course,
five-shilling dinners of the present-day houses, which
cater, often so indifferently and inefficiently, for a much
vaster traffic. Of course, there were exceptions, and the
little inns in remote districts off the main highways must
have offered a very simple fare indeed. But generally
there was a cheerful and vigorous smack about the
coaching and inn life of the early nineteenth century, as
though the roads inspired their officers, from the red-
faced coachman to the bandy-legged ostler, with a spirit
of buoyant optimism rather similar to that with which
the sea inspires its sailors. And if coach travel was often
a long, dull, slow business, it had its romantic thrill for
the more observant, which finds expression in many
delightful contemporary accounts, of which a few have
been included in the fifth chapter.

While many old alehouses retain their original settles
and tables, the fine fittings of the larger inns were very
largely replaced by a mass of ponderous Victorian
mahogany, quite pleasant in its earlier stages, but declining
in quality as the century advanced. *The Royal Hotel* at
Southend a few years ago preserved a remarkable range
of Regency furniture, and the work of Chippendale could
be seen in *The Swan* at Newport Pagnell. *The Lygon Arms*
at Broadway (9), and a few others of its type, are of
course practically museums, in which the pieces have
been carefully and tastefully collected over many years.
But these are exceptions. In the ordinary run of inns,
everyone will remember the type which seems to have
been furnished almost entirely, over a long period of
years, from local mansion sales, in which one's bedroom
probably contains faded water-colours made by faded
and forgotten spinsters, pretty samplers worked by pink-
cheeked children in awful schoolrooms, and formidable
bedsteads that have witnessed a procession of 'county'
births, deaths, and marriages. There are some corridors
in *The Star* at Worcester that form a regular encyclo-
paedia of nineteenth-century taste. Some of these hap-
hazard interiors are very delightful, but they should

43 THE GREAT WHITE HORSE, IPSWICH. The scene of
Mr Pickwick's nocturnal adventure

44 THE GEORGE, PORTSMOUTH. Familiar to generations
of naval officers

45 THE ROYAL CLARENCE, BRIDGWATER, SOMERSET.
A Regency stucco hotel of *circa* 1810

46 THE GEORGE, GRANTHAM, LINCOLNSHIRE. A large and
dignified Georgian inn of *circa* 1780

not be confused with the shoddy bleakness of much later furnishing, that seems to consider any gimcrack Edwardian rubbish, picked up cheap as a job lot, a suitable background for a ten-and-sixpenny bed-and-breakfast. But while everybody has stayed the night at inns that they have left the next morning in a rage, it must be conceded that the large companies that are now absorbing so many old houses all over the country, such as Trust Houses and the P.R.H.A., have done much to improve the standard of comfort and to lower the scale of charges, though there is still more to be done in this direction.

As regards planning, no definite system was ever established for larger inns other than that of providing a yard with sets of lodgings grouped around it, and an inner yard for stabling and waggons. *The Haycock* at Wansford (25), for example, is a finely typical example of late seventeenth-century planning on the lines of a mansion. With the Georgian period, it became necessary to provide easy ingress through a tall archway for stage coaches, which generally made their way out through a gate in the further yard to avoid turning. On one side of the coach entrance would be generally a large dining-room for passengers; and on the other side was the coach office, and a passage connecting with the bar and coffee-room. The drawing-room reserved for ladies was on the first floor. This arrangement was generally followed in all parts of the country, but there were some notable exceptions, and *The Stamford Hotel* (33), planned early in the nineteenth century by John Linnell Bond, has many of the characteristics of the modern hotel. It is entered through a vaulted central vestibule, which provides a glimpse of the graceful geometrical staircase, lit from above by a fine lantern. To the left and right of the vestibule are respectively the coffee-room and morning-room, and on the left of the staircase is the office with its glazed screen. The arched coach entrance is on the extreme left of the façade, leading into a series of rectangular courtyards, around the first of which stand the heavy stone ranges of an older eighteenth-century building.

The Stamford Hotel is a landmark in the nineteenth-century transformation of the coaching inn. Space forbids more than the mention of a number of others in which these changes are crystallised, but, in addition to *The Swan* at Bedford and *The White Hart* at Salisbury already mentioned, there is *The Grosvenor* at Shaftesbury, with its Tuscan order; *The London Inn* at Exeter, with its Doric portico; *The Royal* at Plymouth, built by that exuberant local architect, John Foulston, who specialised in all the styles from Gothic to Egyptian; *The Royal* at Falmouth; *The Royal Clarence* at Bridgwater (45); *The George* at Portsmouth (44); *The Lion* at Guildford (47); *The Queen's* at Cheltenham; *The Old Ship* at Brighton (48); *The Antelope* and *The King's Arms* (22) at Dorchester; *The Bull* at Rochester (39, 40), made famous by Dickens; and many others. Most of them were designed frankly as public buildings, in the solid, honest-to-God Doric, Ionic, or Corinthian of the time; the snug English tradition of the 'home from home' was fast fading. But with the coming of the railways, the importance, and the dignity, and indeed the custom of these majestic houses began to wane. The new 'station hotels' were taking their place. Gilbert Scott's Gothic masterpiece of inconvenient planning, *The Midland Grand* at St. Pancras Station, is the apotheosis of the new ideal. Across the road, at King's Cross, *The Great Northern Hotel* is in the old Georgian tradition of architectural style, but it looks like an overgrown posting-house bent into the shape of a crescent. Philip C. Hardwick's *Great Western Hotel* at Paddington, and Edward Myddleton Barry's *Charing Cross Hotel*, herald a new era in Victorian hotel architecture, and *The Russell Hotel*, London, *The Central* at Glasgow, *The Midland* at Leeds, and many and many a hydro in many and many a watering-place are examples of this architecture at its latest and worst.

After a time when most hotels seem to have emulated Eastbourne *in excelsis*, a Louis–Ritz style was invented which has served very well until the present day. And now fashions are changing once again. It is a far cry from *The Tabard* to *The Cumberland*.

47 THE LION, GUILDFORD, SURREY. An Early Victorian
frontage on the steep High Street

48 THE OLD SHIP, BRIGHTON, SUSSEX.
Regency bow-windows and ironwork

49 THE ROYAL OAK, WINSFORD, SOMERSET. A pretty thatched
inn on the fringe of Exmoor

III

THE SMALL INN AND ALEHOUSE

While the large coaching inn at any period was of a type that varied little throughout the country, save in the brick, timber, or local stone of which it was constructed, the smaller inn and alehouse provided, and still provide, a much more exact register of the character and usage of individual districts. The greater inns for the most part represent a slow growth by stages through the centuries, however emphatically their frontages proclaim a single period. The smaller inns, modestly typical of the building conditions of their locality, seldom shared the ambitions of their big brothers. Their function was to provide casual refreshment and good cheer—not the organised comfort required by the passenger in the age before steam. While the larger inn catered principally for a shifting and impersonal population engaged on the serious and uncomfortable business of travel, the alehouse supplied a purely local need, boasting its own circle of regular customers, its own collection of taproom wags and characters, and frequently its own specialities in the way of food, drink, games, and amusement. Often it took pride in being a rendezvous of local sportsmen, as can be seen from signs such as *The Horse and Hounds* and *The Anglers' Rest* all over the country; and often, again, it set out to cater for a special line of custom, as in *The Waggon and Horses*, *The Bricklayers' Arms*, and later, *The Railway Tavern*. At the cross-roads of England many of these smaller houses still stand, modest but inviting, disdaining the attractions of Neon lights and touring-club signs, but nevertheless offering a simple welcome to the traveller who chances to stop his car and enter by the tap-room door.

The interior, often enough, remains little changed from the time when Morland loved to portray the scene at these homely places of entertainment. There is still, probably, the great fireplace, with its inglenook, and the

hooks along its upper beam for the pewter tankards.
There are still the tall wooden settles of the chimney-
corner, with the scrubbed deal tables and stools that
have done service there since time immemorial. There
may even be the old flagged floor, and the dark raftered
ceiling, also with its hooks for hanging the flitches of
home-cured bacon. Perhaps an occasional ornament
remains from the old days, such as a Georgian grandfather
clock, or a Staffordshire figure; and there is the inevitable
cork dart board, painted in gay coloured circles, on

THE OLD CHIMNEY-CORNER AT 'THE UNION INN,' FLYFORD FLAVELL,
WORCESTERSHIRE

which local talent displays its prowess each evening from
'opening-time' on. The clutter of modern looking-glasses,
ash-trays, display-cards, and ornaments of every kind,
thoughtfully provided by Big Business, and loudly
proclaiming its slogans, scarcely detracts from the sleepy
charm of the effect; even the glutinous waltz-music
oozing through the loud-speaker from a Jewish trio in
a London grill-room seems, in some remarkable way,
in keeping. The tradition of centuries is not lightly
disturbed, and these alehouse parlours are as intimately
connected with the history and fortunes of their villages
as are even the manor-houses and the churches.

50 THE VILLAGE TAPROOM. An interior at the Crooked House
Inn, Himley, Staffordshire

51 THE RED LION, GRANTCHESTER, CAMBRIDGESHIRE.
A Georgian alehouse in Rupert Brooke's favourite village

52 THE WHITE HORSE, KERSEY, SUFFOLK. A village alehouse
in East Anglia

53 THE FLYING HORSE, BOUGHTON ALUPH, KENT. A pleasant
little building in the 'Tudor' of 1840

54 THE NEW INN, BICKLEIGH, DEVON. Built of the local cob
and thatch—with even a thatched sign

55 THE STAR, ALFRISTON, SUSSEX. One of the most perfect surviving
specimens of the timber inn of the fifteenth century

Some of the earliest of the smaller inns were those placed by the Church on the medieval pilgrim routes, such as the beautiful fifteenth-century *Star* at Alfriston (55), which belonged to the Abbey of Battle. Others sprang up along the tracks frequented by pack-horse trains, and these, even though rebuilt, can often be identified by such names as *The Nag's Head* and *The Pack Horse*, as on the route across the Chilterns from the Thames Valley to Dunstable. Such establishments were built purely as places of refreshment, and were legally prohibited from providing lodging for strangers until as late as the seventeenth century, though it would not seem that this law was ever very stringently enforced. The fare that they provided, however, was generally ample and wholesome, inspiring the Carolean traveller, Fynes Moryson, to his famous encomium, that "the World affoords not such Innes as England hath, either for good and cheape entertainement after the Guests owne pleasure, or for humble attendance on passengers, yea in very poore Villages, where if Curculio of Plautus should see the thatched houses, he would fall into a fainting of his spirits, but if he should smell the variety of meates, his starveling look would be much cheared."

By the time of Pepys, the regulations against alehouse accommodation seem either to have been relaxed or to have fallen into abeyance. For the traveller intrepid enough to put up at one of these houses, however, the conditions were hardly ideal, and the diarist records good-humouredly how he and his party were forced to lie the night at an alehouse on Salisbury Plain, where, on rising, they found "the beds good but lousy, which made us merry" (*vide* p. 77). At *The Rose and Crown* at Nether Stowey, the 'Water Poet' Taylor was not only baffled in all his efforts to procure supper, but throughout the night was subjected to the attack of "an Ethopian army of fleas" (*vide* p. 76). Moreover, at this period, dirt and discomfort were not the only misfortunes that could befall chance wayfarers. Certain small inns and alehouses had very unsavoury reputations indeed, and their 'chamberlains' and ostlers were suspected, with a good deal of

justification, of tipping off highwaymen and robbers
when they sniffed a likely prey. Sometimes even the
landlords were in the pay of these hawks of the road,
as the notorious highwayman Clavel asserted in his
Recantation of an Ill Ledde Life. The *Unicorn* at Bruton
and the inn at Shepton Mallett were both suspected in
this connection, while *The Leopard's Head* at Ware had a
"privye place" for hiding stolen goods and fugitives from
the law.

The small country inns and alehouses of England
number legion, and it is impossible to do justice to any
but a select few in this short chapter. The photographs
give some idea of their variety, which is infinite; and
they are to be found along the highways, sometimes
forming the centres of straggling communities of small
cottages, sometimes set down alone and out of sight of
other human habitation. A few are still even extraordinarily lonely in their situation, as *The Cat and the
Fiddle*, perched at sixteen hundred feet on the crest
of the heathery moors above Buxton, the remote little
Travellers' Rest (56) in a severe fold of the Kirkstone
Pass among the Cumberland Fells, *The Saltersgate Inn* in
the Cleveland Hills on the road to Whitby, with its peat
fire that never goes out, to welcome moorland travellers,
and many others. The larger villages and small towns can
generally boast quite a number of them in addition to
their principal inns, while the lesser streets of county
towns and cathedral cities often literally teem with them.
Aylesbury, for instance, is reputed to have a larger
percentage of inns in proportion to its population than
any town in England, and in such a city as Norwich they
are to be seen at every corner (72), pleasant old buildings,
for the most part, that have faithfully served the same
purpose through many centuries.

The Cat and Fiddle at Hinton Admiral in Hampshire (57)
is a delightful example of the wayside alehouse of
Southern England, a low plastered building that nevertheless contrives to accommodate two storeys beneath its
overhanging roof of thatch. In the same county, the
little thatched inn at Cadnam (58) is charmingly typical

THE TRAVELLERS' REST, KIRKSTONE PASS, WESTMORLAND.   This
lonely Lakeland inn, at 1480 feet, is seen in the distance at the
junction of the two roads

57 THE CAT AND FIDDLE, HINTON ADMIRAL, HAMPSHIRE. A delightful wayside alehouse

58 CADNAM, HAMPSHIRE. A wayside alehouse in the New Forest

59   THE LEATHER BOTTLE, COBHAM, KENT.   Where Mr Tracey Tupman fled to

of the hamlet inn, forming the central feature of a pleasant group of cottages of similar type in a pretty clearing of the New Forest. Typical small Surrey inns, dating from the fifteenth or sixteenth century and still preserving their original timberings, are *The Old Bell* at Oxted and *The Leather Bottle* at Cobham (59), while other inns of the South-East are to be found pleasantly faced with rosy tiles, as *The Crown* at Chiddingfold (74) and

A VANTAGE-POINT OF THE COTSWOLDS. THE LITTLE 'FISH INN'
ABOVE BROADWAY

The White Hart at Witley (83). Essex and Suffolk have their innumerable small inns, built of timber and finished externally with plaster or weather-boarding, such as *The Angel* at Lavenham (109) and *The Fleece* at Brentwood (84), while in Hertfordshire and Bedfordshire the buildings are for the most part of brick, as *The Blue Boy* at Hertford, which adjoins, and is contemporary with, the Bluecoat School, and *The Red Lion* at Water End, near Gaddesden, with its prim bay windows. Half-timber runs riot in the Western Midlands, and here, among a crowd of fine old houses, often patterned more elaborately than zebras, it is

H

only possible to mention *The Falcon* and *The Bear and Billet* (66) at Chester, *The Wheatsheaf* and *The Bell* (67) at Tewkesbury, *The King's Arms* at Ombersley (61), *The Talbot* at Chaddesley Corbett (62), and *The Swan* at Bridgnorth (64). But to enumerate all the varieties of inn buildings it would be necessary to enter upon a survey of local types in English architecture, a subject of considerable complexity, far beyond the scope of these pages. Let it suffice that the little inns represent as truth-

THE 'FALCON INN,' CHESTER

fully as any other kind of building the development and ramifications of this architecture at every period, and are consequently just as worthy of study as the churches, the manor-houses, or the castles.

But in the country the alehouses are dying out. Hertfordshire still seems to have more of them than anywhere else, though at Waltham Abbey, little more than thirty years ago, we can remember a whole row of them in the market-place, from which the licences have been gradually withdrawn, until now there are only three left, where formerly there were twelve or more, to compete with the

60 THE SIR GARNET WOLSELEY, NORWICH. Under the shadow
of the great church of St Peter Mancroft, this inn does a thriving
business on market days

61 THE KING'S ARMS, OMBERSLEY, WORCESTERSHIRE

62 THE TALBOT, CHADDESLEY CORBETT, WORCESTERSHIRE.
Fine half-timber inns in Western-Midland villages

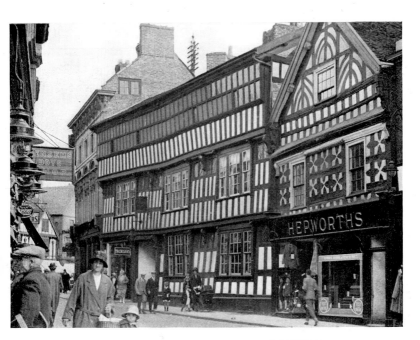

63   THE CROWN, NANTWICH, CHESHIRE

64   THE SWAN, BRIDGNORTH, SHROPSHIRE.
Two picturesque half-timber frontages in old Welsh-Border towns

66 THE BEAR AND BILLET, CHESTER. The famous half-timber inn by the Bridge Gate, once the

65 THE GARRICK, STRATFORD-ON-AVON, WAR-WICKSHIRE. Forming a pleasant half-timber

larger houses. It is strangely enough London that has
retained more of its old alehouses than any other great
city, though, as has been seen, the larger inns have for
the most part vanished. These alehouses (or shall we
avoid a possible accusation of archaism and call them
'pubs'?) have generally managed to adapt themselves,
more or less, to changing social conditions. Thus, the
dividing up of the counter into a 'public' and a 'saloon'
bar (to say nothing of such social subtleties as the 'private
bar,' 'ladies' wine bar,' and 'jug and bottle') was a result
of the industrial era. Foremen did not like to drink with
their men, so they paid an extra halfpenny and drank
with other foremen. There are even, in some of the more
Victorian public-houses, the old movable screens over
the bars, whose opaque glass panels can be swivelled
about so that one can avoid the eye of a social inferior
in a neighbouring compartment.

The types and idiosyncrasies of the London pubs would
provide material for a fascinating study that would fill
many volumes, though one would have to take to drink
in earnest to be able to bring it anywhere near completion
in a normal lifetime. Most of the nicest ones are run
either by retired athletes (principally boxers) or retired
music-hall artists, and the walls of these are generally
decorated with an array of inscribed photographs of
bruisers, soubrettes, acrobats, racing-cyclists, red-nosed
comedians, sporting peers, and the like. Most of the
public-houses of central London have their own regular
clientèles; thus Art, having shifted its quarters from
Chelsea to Bloomsbury, is to be found taking its ease to
the music of an electric piano in *The Fitzroy* in Charlotte
Street, while the sporting world patronises the bars of
a famous retired heavyweight champion near Leicester
Square, and the French Colony crams itself nightly, as
tightly as sardines in a tin, into a little public-house
behind the Palace Theatre in Soho. A 'pub-crawl' around
London is one of the best introductions that can be given
a visiting foreigner to the charming vagaries of the
English capital—that is, provided his stomach is strong
enough to absorb unlimited quantities of English bitter

beer. From the cosmopolitan elegance of *The Running Horse* in Mayfair to a Saturday-night shindy in the West India Dock Road is a long trail, but one that every true Londoner should follow at least once in his lifetime if he is to gain a broader appreciation of his fellow-citizens.

The Georgian taverns of London can be studied in a number of fine examples that remain to us intact, though these for the most part have developed almost exclusively into eating-houses. True, many of the more famous ones have vanished, such as *The Boar's Head* in Cheapside, and *Dolly's Tavern*, which took its name from the old cook of the place, whose portrait Gainsborough painted. No trace remains of *The Three Cranes* in Thames Street, a famous meeting-place of wits in the reign of James I; "A pox o' these pretenders to wit," wrote Ben Jonson in *Bartholomew Fair*, "your Three Cranes, Mitre and Mermaid men, not a corn of true thought, not a grain of right mustard amongst them all." Pepys dined at this tavern with some poor relations, and recorded: "We all went over to the Three Cranes Taverne, and (though the best room in the house) in such a narrow dogg-hole were we crammed (and I believe we were near forty) and it made me loathe my company and victuals, and a sorry poor dinner it was too." The bowed Elizabethan front of *The Sir Paul Pindar* is preserved intact in the Victoria and Albert Museum, London. This, though formerly the house of the great city merchant of that name, became a tavern in 1811.

It seems to have been part of the scheme of the old coffee-houses and taverns to play hide-and-seek with their customers in obscure courtyards and alleys, hidden away from the main thoroughfares of business. Thus it is with *The Mitre* in Mitre Court, the old *Simpson's* near the Mansion House, and *The Cheshire Cheese* in Wine Office Court off Fleet Street. This latter, with its famous pudding, its stuffed parrot, and its memories of Samuel Johnson, Charles Dickens, and a host of journalists, lawyers, and literary men, has become a national institution, and a place of pilgrimage for the devout of many nations. And there is compensation for the dis-

67 THE BELL, TEWKESBURY, GLOUCESTERSHIRE. The famous
Elizabethan inn flanking the Abbey Church

68　THE RUNNING FOOTMAN, MAYFAIR.　Built as a discreet Early
Victorian *rendezvous* for the plush-breeches aristocracy of Berkeley Square

comfort of its cramped wooden settles in the excellence and plenty of its fare. The place is, indeed, as much a part of London as the Tower, Westminster Abbey, or the November fogs.

Many of the old inns and alehouses of the London villages have survived, though often badly 'modernised' by the breweries which own them (a process that generally consists in attempting to make them look medieval where before they were plainly Georgian, and Georgian where before they were honestly Victorian). Others have

THE INTERIOR OF THE OLD 'CHESHIRE CHEESE' IN WINE
OFFICE COURT

entirely vanished, such as *The Monster*, with its popular tea-garden, that stood at the corner of St. George's Row and Buckingham Palace Road, and probably derived its unusual name from the fact that the land originally belonged to the Monastery, or Abbey of Westminster; *The Sun*, with its rival gardens, only a stone's-throw away; and *The White Horse* and *Black Lion* in Chelsea. Such famous Georgian inns as *The Angel* at Islington and *The Elephant and Castle* have changed their honest brick for Lyons and terracotta, but a little further afield there is *The Chandos Arms* at Edgware, *The Ferry Boat* at Tottenham, *The Old Crown Inn* at Dulwich, *The Plough* in Lordship Lane, *The Spaniards* and *Jack Straw's Castle* at

I

Hampstead, and the beautiful old *Mitre*, flanking Sir Edwin Lutyens' new bridge at Hampton Court, where the food is so good. At Greenwich, only the Early Victorian *Ship* remains on the west side of the hospital; its opposite number on the east side, *The Trafalgar Tavern*, with its charming treillage balconies overlooking the river, is now derelict and condemned. Dickens mentions these inns in *Our Mutual Friend*, and well within the last century

THE BAR-PARLOUR OF 'THE TROUT' AT GODSTOW

it was still the custom for the Government and Opposition to be rowed once a year down the river to Greenwich in separate barges, there to partake of the whitebait dinners for which the place was famous, the Government at *The Ship* and the Opposition at *The Trafalgar*. Whistler discovered the charm of *The Grapes* in Limehouse Reach (69), with its crazy timber galleries rising above the untidy river foreshore, and perpetuated it in an etching; and this house was also the original of the famous *Six Jolly Fellowship Porters* in *Our Mutual Friend*. Further up-river, at Wapping, are *The Turk's Head*, *The Town of Ramsgate*, and *The Prospect of Whitby*, also over-

69 THE GRAPES, LIMEHOUSE, LONDON. Etched by Whistler, and
the Thameside original of Dickens' 'Six Jolly Fellowship Porters'

70 THE LONDON APPRENTICE, ISLEWORTH, MIDDLESEX.
A fine old Thameside inn in a London Village

71 THE DOVES, HAMMERSMITH, LONDON. One of the Capital's
few open-air drinking-places, overlooking the Thames

72 THE BRITON'S ARMS, ELM HILL, NORWICH. In a quiet
corner of the ancient cathedral city

73 THE ALEHOUSE HEARTH. An interior at *The Castle*,
Old Sarum, Wiltshire

74 THE ALEHOUSE BENCH. Outside the beautiful tile-hung *Crown*
at Chiddingfold, Surrey

BAR INTERIOR, THE 'POMFRET ARMS,'
TOWCESTER

looking the water; and beyond Westminster, the old
waterfronts of Chiswick and Hammersmith preserve
some delightful old houses, such as *The Black Lion*, with
its garden of snapdragons and open-air tables, where
Mr. A. P. Herbert plays skittles, and *The Doves*, with its
memories of William Morris, where one can also sit
drinking in the open, overlooking the water (71). At
Isleworth, still a real London village caught in a fold
of the Thames, the Georgian weatherboarded *London
Apprentice* has a delightfully nautical air (70).

But there is no end to English alehouses, either in
London or in the country, and this short chapter cannot
pretend to do more than scrape the surface of a vast and
fertile field of study. Modern restrictions, and the baneful
activities of Dora, are doing their best to stifle the pleasant
companionable tradition of these places, but I somehow
do not feel that they will succeed. Let the justices refuse
them a licence and petty legislation ring them a curfew
at ten, there will still be English people left who will
prefer sitting cosily over a fire in a bar-parlour, with a
drink at their elbow and in good company, to gaping at
Garbo in the Hollywood splendour of the local 'Super.'
As long as these sort of people remain, there will always
be an alehouse tucked away for them somewhere handy
but unobtrusive around a corner, defying the cold dis-
approval of the mandarins responsible for the mass-
production of our future leisure.

THE MEDIEVAL SIGN OF AN EVERGREEN BUSH.
FROM A XIVTH-CENTURY MANUSCRIPT

75 THE DUN COW, SHREWSBURY. A blatant example of crude faking. The plaster front of this charming little gabled inn has been adorned with painted zebra stripes to suggest half-timber

76   THE OLD CORNER CUPBOARD, WINCHCOMB, GLOUCESTERSHIRE.   A beautiful

77 THE BUTT AND OYSTER, PIN MILL, SUFFOLK. A resort of fishermen, overlooking
the Orwell Estuary

· 78, 79 CASTLE COMBE, WILTSHIRE. (*Above*) A small alehouse, and (*below*)
the *Castle Inn*, in one of the most exquisite old villages in England

80 THE FOX AND HOUNDS, STANTON, BERKSHIRE

81 THE FEATHERS, EAST HAGBOURNE, BERKSHIRE.
Two picturesque village inns in the Vale of the White Horse

82 THE HALF MOON, CHARLWOOD, SURREY. A typical English village group, though now almost absorbed by Greater London

83 THE WHITE HART, WITLEY, SURREY. A delightful example of the local tile-hanging

84 THE FLEECE, BRENTWOOD, ESSEX. On the Colchester Road

85 THE WHITE HART, DORCHESTER, OXFORDSHIRE. In the
Thameside village on the Oxford Road

86 THE FERRY INN, HORNING, NORFOLK. A little inn on the
Broads. Notice the stacks of drying reeds

87 THE ROSE AND CROWN, STANTON, SUFFOLK. A rather
eccentric frontage, with an ambitious ironwork sign

88 THE GREEN DRAGON, ALDERBURY, WILTSHIRE. A village
inn on Salisbury Plain

89 THE OLD GEORGE, SHOREHAM, KENT. With a distant
glimpse of the North Downs

90 THE CROWN, SARRE, KENT. Or a jolly Sunday evening in Thanet

91 THE EIGHT BELLS, HATFIELD, HERTFORDSHIRE. In spite of its demure appearance, this Georgian alehouse was chosen by Dickens as a haunt of the savage Bill Sykes

92 THE BELL, THETFORD, NORFOLK. A pleasant building of the seventeenth century, in characteristic East-Anglian plaster

IV

INN NAMES AND THEIR LORE

The subject of the inn names, and the signs and notice-boards by which they are displayed to public view, is immensely wide and varied, and has its own fascination and attraction. In them are crystallised many of the facets of social life and history from the long past of our land. It can only be lightly touched upon here, and indeed deserves separate treatment, for though Larwood and Hotten's survey of 1866 abounds in rambling information, there is room for an adequate review with modern

FIFTEENTH-CENTURY WOODEN DEVICE AT 'THE SWAN,' CLARE, SUFFOLK, PROBABLY ORIGINALLY PLACED UNDER AN ORIEL WINDOW

illustrations. The sign goes back to classical times, and the most ancient device of the wine-seller is the Bush, as enshrined in the proverb still current. It appears in medieval manuscripts (p. 50), and with the adoption of heraldic and similar devices was relegated to the humbler alehouse, as appears when Taylor the water poet, in his survey of the hostelries within three miles of London in the time of Charles I, lists some inns having but the bush, as among "Greenwich Tavernes"—"one with a bush onely, by Deptford Bridge. . . ." In medieval times came the display of many subjects connected with the Church, and such figures borrowed from heraldry as the Helmet and Crown, Unicorn, White Hart, Mermaid, and Red or Golden Lion, and the Chequers (100), a device found in Pompei and possibly derived from the chequer-board used in money calculations. A few medieval devices remain carved in wood, as at *The Swan* at Clare, Suffolk.

Similarly the idea of the rebus was obtained, such as the bolt piercing the tun, for Bolton, changed in time to Bolt and Tun; of which a variant is found in *The War-Bill-in-Tun*, at Warbleton, Sussex, or again, hare and a bottle, for Harbottle. Then there are portraits of kings and famous men, views of castles, ships, griffins and dragons, angels, saints and devils. The Crusaders, perhaps, favoured *The Trip to Jerusalem*, *Saracen's Head*, *The Fleur-de-Lys*, or *The Turk's Head*.

It was natural to take names of animals, from the camel to the cow, the bird tribe from the eagle to the dove, the vegetable kingdom, from the lily to the artichoke, terms from countryside and coast, and combine them with the tools of agriculture and trade. In names human nature loves to express its fundamental qualities, and thus we meet signs warlike, convivial, industrial, humorous, grotesque, bombastic, snobbish, storytelling, and moralising. By the seventeenth century most of the regular well-known terms were in common use, as appears in Taylor's survey, and in a perambulation from Whitehall to the Tower, preserved in the Harleian MS. 6850, fol. 31, which enumerates 37. It is very interesting to trace the parallel between inn names and the devices on horse brasses; a considerable number of subjects are identical, such as the Lion, Castle, Swan, Cock, Fox, Ship, Sun, Plough, Windmill, and Horseshoes in varying numbers. Many of the representations on the martingales would make excellent signs if enlarged and painted or modelled. Some of these names incorporate queer corruptions, or reminiscences of historical events or customs; thus *The Bull and Mouth* is really the Boulogne (Harbour) Mouth; *The Swan with Two Necks* might be Nicks or Notches on the bill, to denote ownership, though the two-necked Swan continued a popular sign, in spite of the suggestion of the 'double bill.' The Pelican at Speenhamland was the subject of a well-known lampoon by eighteenth-century wits "from its enormous bill." The frequent use of the sign King's Head or King's Arms in the Restoration period did not pass unnoticed by the wits, the common saying being: "If the King's

93   THE FOUR SWANS, WALTHAM CROSS, HERTFORDSHIRE.   Showing the famous
Eleanor Cross and ' beam ' sign

94 THE FOX AND HOUNDS, BARLEY, HERTFORDSHIRE.
An attractive 'beam' sign spanning the Old North Road

Head is empty, the King's Arms are full." The most amusing transformation is *The Devil and Bag o' Nails* (the second name still found in London) from a Satyr and Bacchanals; though some think it is an argot impression of the representation of *The Blackamoor's Head and Woolsack*. That *The Goat and Compasses* is from "God Encompasseth Us" is doubtful; the compasses are more likely to be masonic, and *The Globe and Compasses*, still found, is possibly derived from the Joiner's arms. But there are conflicting derivations for most of these curious designations. *The Case is Altered* may refer to a local change, or incorporate the Nathan–David-like incident of Edmund Plowden, the Elizabethan lawyer, and the farmer's cow gored by his bull. The words also appear in a saying of his about the mass. *La Belle Sauvage* might point to Pocohontas, or be older as *The Savage and Bell*, in which form it has appeared on signs. *The Axe and Battle* might be from the Battleaxe, and it is suggested that *The Leg and Seven Stars* is really the League of Seven Stars, or United Provinces.

The Feathers or *Plume of Feathers* commemorates successive Princes of Wales, and *The Royal Oak* recalls Charles II's escape at Boscobel after the Battle of Worcester, but *The British Oak* or *Brave Old Oak* refer to the national tree. The still popular name of *The Talbot* represents a large type of sporting dog; it was adopted as a sign by Chaucer's *Tabard* of Southwark in 1676. It is good that *The Running Footman* survives in May-fair (68), and London still keeps a couple of *Two Chairmen* in the West End, reminiscent like the iron link-extinguishers of the days of the sedan. *The Eagle and Child*, popular round Derbyshire, is connected with a crest of the Stanleys, the Earls of Derby, recalling the legend of a child found at the foot of a tree in which an eagle had nested. *The Bear and Ragged Staff* is of course the time-honoured badge of the Earls of Warwick.

John Taylor, who did so much to record the inns of the early seventeenth century, tried his hand at inn-keeping as well as professional touring and the water-man's job. He first kept a tavern at Oxford, and for his fantastic and scurrilous attacks on the Parliamentary party was made a Yeoman of the Guard. After the loss of Oxford in 1645 he took *The Crown* in Phoenix Alley, Long Acre, and showed his obstinate royalism in re-christening it *The Mourning Crown* after Charles the First was beheaded. This was soon stigmatised as 'malignant' and its removal enforced; he then substituted *The Poet's Head*, showing his own portrait, inscribed:—

> There's many a head stands for a sign
> Then, gentle reader, why not mine?

and on the reverse:—

> Though I deserve not, I desire
> The laurel wreath, the poet's hire,

issuing of course a characteristic rhyming pamphlet, an excellent piece of publicity, which includes the following:—

> Now if my picture's drawing can prevayle
> 'Twill draw my friends to me, and I'll draw ale.
> Two strings are better to a bow than one;
> And poeting does me small good alone.
> So ale alone yields but small good to me,
> Except it have some spice of poesie.

The warrant issued against him for treasonable con-duct was never executed, and he died at his inn. *The Mourning Crown* occurs later, as well as *Charles the Second's Head* and *The Merry Monarch*.

The Haycock at Wansford has already been mentioned and illustrated (25, and pp. 16, 37). In its recent reopening as an inn after a period of retirement it parallels *The Rose Revived* on the upper Thames (116). It forms an attractive composition with the broach spire of the church and the fine old bridge, now by-passed by the Great North Road, over an imposing reinforced concrete erection. The tale by which the place got its unique name tells that a countryman, fallen asleep on a haycock further up the river, was carried away by the rising of the stream, and, awakened by his queer craft bumping against the bridge piers, inquired where he was. On being told "At Wansford," he asked, "What, in England?" This incident is painted on the sign, preserved during the tenure as a private house, and now again in use. Taylor, however, gives a different and less appropriate version:—

> On a haycock sleeping soundly
> The river rose, and took me roundly
> Down the current; people cried,
> As along the stream I hied.
> "Where away?" quoth they, "From Greenland?"
> "No; from Wansford Bridge in England."

At the beginning of the nineteenth century, as was to be expected in a period of protracted warfare, the signs took on direct allusions to naval and military victories and heroes. This and later outbursts of fervid patriotism are reflected in such terms as *The Wooden Walls of Old England*, *British Banner*, *True Briton*, *Salamanca*, *Alma*, *Rock of Gibraltar*, *Hero of Maida* or *Moultan*, with, curious survival of Napoleonic rancour, *The Antigallican*, and a range of Admirals, Peer-Generals, and other famous or local Dukes, Earls, Marquises, etc., even including one to *Lord Byron*. To this stage belong *The Rifleman*, *Carabineers*, *Loyal Volunteer*, and their variants. *Bishop Blaize* and *Bishop Bonner* are also among those honoured. By the year 1820 coaching and innkeeping reached the height of prosperity; hence is found the reason for such signs as *Coach and Horses*, *Chaise and Pair*, *The Quicksilver Mail*, *The Telegraph*, *The Comet*, *The Regent*, and *The Wagon*. George III in effigy gave place to the rubicund features of George IV, and later to the chubby portrait of the Sailor King. Finally, when the harsh clank of the locomotive echoed down through the country from Stockton and Darlington, and later the London and Birmingham line astonished the Midland countryside, we find such signs as *The Live and Let Live*, *The Locomotive*, *The Engine Inn*, marking the change and proving to a disquieted world that the roads and inns were about to be neglected. The earlier developments of communication appear in the *Canal*, *Navigation*, and *Tram* inns. A tavern called *The E.U.R.* at Ipswich is possibly named after the rudimentary Eastern Union Railway. Coast and River-side Inns naturally ring the changes on nautical associations, such as *The Safe Harbour, Welcome Sailor, China Ship, Sloop, Steam Packet, Oyster Smack, Black Buoy, Sea Witch,* and *Fish and Eels.*

Intensive industry was now entering into its domain and, in consequence, publicans were not slow to encourage artisan customers. Thus we find *Bricklayers' Arms, Gardeners' Arms, Graveldiggers', Miners', Weavers',* and even *Pyrotechnists'* and *Blockers' Arms,* with a host of other callings too numerous to index. In smelting districts occur *The Forge, Hammer, The Three Furnaces,* and *The Old Engine* (stationary of course). A number have the prefix *Jolly,* as in *Jolly Weavers, Threshers, Butchers,* or *Jovial Collier,* though the term is more often applied to Farmers, Sailors, Sportsmen, and Cricketers. These stand in sharp contrast to the Arms of the Family of the Squire or Lord, frequently forming, in the elaborate armorial quarterings painted on the faded sign, exactly similar to the hatchments preserved in churches, the only commemoration of a vanished grandeur. It is a pleasant custom to honour the implements of the local industry, as the tools are carved on the bench ends at Altarnun and elsewhere in Cornwall. We get *The Axe and Cleaver, Malt Shovel, Stocking Frame, Hand and Shears, Drill, Three Hammers, Shuttles,* and *Beetle and Wedge,* the first of these referring not to the insect but the huge wooden mallet. Combinations are *The Plough and Shuttle, Plough and Sail,* etc.

The idea of conviviality and good fellowship occasionally crops up, but not as often as might be expected, with such names as *The Bank of Friendship, Invitation, Three Cronies, Old Tippling Philosopher, Happy Returns, Horn of Plenty, Castle* or *Cottage of Comfort, Slow and Easy,* and *Smoker. The Old Fox with his Teeth Drawn* is a temperance inn in Hertfordshire, once *The Fox,* but transformed by a son-in-law of Sir Wilfred Lawson, champion of temperance. *The Land of Liberty* recalls a vanished Chartist experiment. At Upware Ferry in the Fens the inn bears

95 THE BEEHIVE, GRANTHAM, LINCOLNSHIRE.
'Grantham, two rarities are thine!
A lofty steeple and a living sign.'
The 'living sign' consists of a beehive, inhabited by its swarm

96 THE CHEQUERS, TONBRIDGE, KENT. A summer view of the medieval timbered inn, now much restored

round its gable the inscription, *Five Miles from Anywhere, No Hurry*.

But features and aspects of country life naturally fill a large part of the range of inn titles, with names like the *Hayrick, Barley Mow, Ploughboy, Ratcatcher, Dusty Miller, Harvesters, Cow and Pail, Fleece and Woolpack*. There is occasionally a local touch, as in Cheshire *The Cheshire Cheese* and *The Wheatsheaf*, prevalent there as giving the county emblem. *The Beehive* at Grantham (95) with its fully inhabited skep is unique. Many, of course, are connected with the horse and its trappings, such as *The Horse and Rider, Pack Horse, Nag's Head, Horse and Jockey, Bay, Sorrel*, or *Chestnut Horse, Saddle, Whip*, and *Horseshoes* in differing numbers. Sport also accounts for a large number; in addition to the commonest we meet *The Huntsman, Gun, Hare and Hounds, Panting Hart, Hunted Stag, Hit or Miss, Dog* alone, and with *Badger, Bear*, or *Duck, Angler*, and *Fish*. Animals are widely favoured, with those who tend them, as *The Shepherd and Flock, Sow and Pigs, Durham* or *Devon Ox, Kentish Drovers, Ram and Hoggett, Squirrel, Kangaroo, Antelope*, or *Buffalo*, the latter recording a local attempt at acclimatisation near Clun; unusual colours are *The Brown Lion* and *Black Greyhound*. Birds supply the *Cock and Blackbird, Doves, Raven, Swan and Sugarloaf*, and *Three Cranes, Choughs*, or *Pigeons*. Trees and flowers furnish *The Thorn, Ash, Cherry Tree, Acorn, Holly Bush, Myrtle, Mulberry, Rosemary Bush, Orange Tree*, with *The Flowerpot*, Rupert Brooke's Chiltern *Pink and Lily*, and *The Blooming Fuchsia*. Musical instruments are also drawn on, with *The Hautboy and Fiddle, Harp, Trumpet*, and *French Horn*. The latter appears curiously joined, e.g. preceded by *Queen's Head* or *Lion*, or followed by *Half Moon*. From great store of curious combinations may be quoted *The Cat and Custard Pot, Parrot and Punchbowl, Bear and Rummer, Rainbow and Dove, Sun and Whalebone, Apple Tree and Mitre, Crown and Crooked Billet, Queen's Head and Artichoke, Hart and Trumpet*; such idiosyncrasies were commented on in a verse in the *British Apollo* at the start of the eighteenth century :—

I'm amazed at the Signs	The Leg and Seven Stars
As I pass through the Town	The Axe and the Bottle
To see the odd Mixture:	The Tun and the Lute
A Magpie and Crown	The Eagle and Child
The Whale and the Crow	The Shovel and Boot.
The Razor and Hen	

These signs of London taverns are fully discussed in the *Spectator* of April 28, 1710, quoted in Chapter V, p. 78.

The George and Blue Boar was famous in Holborn as the place where the condemned drank on their way to Tyburn, promising to pay on their way back. Its name was long retained in the railway office on the site, and like *Griffin's Green Man and Still* further west has only recently vanished.

A CONVIVIAL SCENE CARVED IN STONE ON 'THE GREENHOUSE INN'
(Y TY GWYRDD), LLANVIHANGEL LLANTARNAM, MONMOUTH-
SHIRE, 1719

A turn towards the antique, strange, or grotesque, is shown in *The Ancient Briton, World Upside Down, Savage, Wild,* or *Green Man, African* or *New Zealand Chief, Wyvern, Griffin, Flying Horse,* and *Dragons* of various hues. Bucolic philosophy is enshrined in the *Labour in Vain,* with two women scrubbing a negro, and Hogarth's famous *Load of Mischief,* a man staggering under the burden of a drunken woman, a monkey, and a magpie. Then there is the *Quiet* or *Good* or *Silent Woman,* with her head under her arm, occasionally called *Headless;* the *Honest Lawyer* is similarly depicted. Hardy uses the sign of *The Quiet Woman* for the inn on Egdon Heath in *The Return of the Native. The Five Alls* is fairly frequent; it differs in the persons and their order, but a typical arrangement is a King: *I rule all;* a Parson: *I pray for all;*

97   THE THREE SWANS, MARKET HARBOROUGH, LEICESTERSHIRE.
A fine Georgian house with a superb ironwork sign

98 THE JOLLY FARMER, FARNHAM, SURREY. This bucolic
frontage conceals the birthplace of Cobbett

a Soldier: *I fight for all*; a Lawyer: *I plead for all*; and John Bull: *I pay for all*, the last painfully apposite to-day. Occasionally a Farmer asserts: *I maintain all*, and the final figure is the Devil: *I take all*. The connection between Church and inn, and something of the medieval outlook on life, is commemorated in a number of inn names. For some reason *The Church* is a common sign in Cheshire, and others give *The Salutation, Catherine Wheel, Friar, Mitre, Christopher*, and *Baptist's Head*, with *The Lamb and Flag* of the Agnus Dei, and the *Angel and Harp*. The *Bell* (67, 92) is a favourite device, in varying numbers up

EIGHTEENTH-CENTURY WROUGHT-IRON DEVICE ONCE AT 'THE FOX,' HUNTINGDON, NOW IN THE VICTORIA AND ALBERT MUSEUM, SOUTH KENSINGTON

to *Eight* (91), though *Ten* and *Twelve* are sometimes found; these with the *Ring* or *Peal o' Bells, Eight Ringers*, and variations may be called after well-known local chimes. Finally the heavens contribute the *Sun*, often *Rising*, and occasionally *Golden* or *in Splendour*, once *in the Sands*, but never Setting, the *Moon*, usually as *Half Moon*, a favourite sign in Flanders, and rarely as *Full Moon*, with differing numbers of *Stars, Five, Six*, or *Seven*; *The Sun, Moon and Seven Stars* is the most complete version.

The sign itself is most frequently painted, but is occasionally fashioned in wrought iron, as at *The Horseshoes* at Mongeham, Kent, Ayot St. Lawrence, Hertfordshire, and elsewhere, and in the sign of farrier's tools in the Nottingham Museum (1752). Carved stone tablets

L

were not uncommon in old London, like the *Greyhound*, drawn by J. W. Archer, the *Adam and Eve* of Newgate Street, and the *Dog and Duck*, but they are now only to be found in museums, like the *Boar's Head*, Eastcheap, of 1668 at the Guildhall, though the Welsh border tablet sketched is still in place after over two hundred years. The pargetted device on the former *Sun* at Saffron Walden is uncertain; the enormous *Bear* at Maidenhead is roughly carved in wood with electric-lit eyes. There is in the

SIGN OF 'THE BULL AND MOUTH,' ST. MARTIN'S-LE-GRAND, NOW IN
THE GUILDHALL MUSEUM, LONDON

Guildhall Museum a *Cock and Bottle* made out of twenty-four blue and white Dutch tiles with an ornamental border. The figure of a Fox has been amusingly and ingeniously fashioned in iron by an eighteenth-century craftsman to serve as a sign for the inn of that name at Huntingdon; it is now in the Victoria and Albert Museum. However, the finest carved signs are *The Bull and Mouth*, from St. Martin's-le-Grand, in the Guildhall Museum, which a couplet connects with the eating exploit of Milo of Crete, and the incomparably magnificent beam sign of *The White Hart* at Scole in Norfolk, the disap-

99   THE CASTLE, BENSON, OXFORDSHIRE.   A fine Georgian
front on the southern Oxford Road

100 THE CHEQUERS, STEYNING, SUSSEX. In a quiet townlet
under the South Downs

pearance of which must ever be lamented; the two porches of the inn have likewise vanished. It extended right across the road, and though doubtless dating, like the house, from 1655, pictured with thorough-paced Elizabethan exuberance a whole panorama of the incident of Diana and Actaeon, with angels, lions, justice, and other figures, including one which turned round to show weather-

THE CARVED WOODEN SIGN OF 'THE WHITE HART,' SCOLE, NORFOLK, NOW DEMOLISHED

changes. The artist's name was Fairchild and the cost was £1,057.

Signs can be attached to or suspended from a beam spanning the road, as at *The George*, Stamford (41), *The Four Swans*, Waltham Cross (93), and the delightfully graphic *Fox and Hounds* at Barley, Hertfordshire (94). This method is nowadays less common than when it excited the derisive wonder of foreign visitors like the

Frenchmen, Misson in 1721, and Grosley in 1765, both of whom were reminded of triumphal arches, while Moritz, in 1782, remarks on "the amazing large signs hanging suspended over the street from great beams; they have the appearance of gateways, but the whole apparatus is intended for nothing more than to tell the inquisitive traveller that there is an inn." The other alternatives are the upright post, the projecting bracket, and the modelled device like the *White Harts* at Salisbury (42) and Dorchester, Dorset, the *Dun Cow* at Salop (75), the *White Bull*, Ribchester (101), and the Ipswich *White Horse* (104).

The first two of these three methods lend themselves to the incorporation of graceful and well-designed wrought-iron work (97, 99). These are but the diminished remains of a richer past, as seen in old pictures of Dartford and Chelmsford, but this country never equalled the elaboration of Tyrolese craftsmanship, as at Sterzing on the Brunner, now Italianised as Vipiteno. Post signs are found at *The White Hart*, Bletchingly, Surrey, and *The Lamb*, Wallingford, with the dismantled *Fountain* from Bedford. Brackets range from the simplest type, like *The Bull* at Redbourn, to the more elaborate workmanship of *The Bull* at Bruton, and the fine *Swan* at Market Harborough (97). Later are the example at Barnet, with its precariously poised modelled Red Lion, and *The Ship* at Mere, poor for all its elaboration; a similar example occurs in Wiltshire at Wylye. The latter two with *The Swan* at Knowle and the East Anglian examples of *The Bull*, Sudbury, and *The Swan* at Harleston are supported by multiple stays.

In the late eighteenth and early nineteenth centuries the production of signs was a recognised industry, the chief centre being Harp Alley, Shoe Lane, where it was possible to purchase bunches of gilded grapes, sugar-loaves, carved lions, busts, canisters, and teapots. In all parts of the country relics from Harp Alley are still to be encountered, sometimes suspended from wrought-iron signs made by local smiths, as at *The Swan*, Bridgnorth (64), and in other cases, as in *The Sugar Loaf* at Dunstable,

swinging above the cornice of the portico. Other forms
of signs were made, for instance, medieval; at *The Angel*
at Grantham (5) and *The George* at Glastonbury (p. 26) a
stone corbel formed part of the building, and on it was
placed the wooden effigy of the angel or saint.

THE IRONWORK SIGN OF 'THE RED LION' ON BARNET HILL

Reference to old songs and ballads of the sixteenth to
the eighteenth centuries proves the signs of inns to have
been a popular theme. There is, for example, the black-
letter tract called *Newes from Bartholomew Fayre*:—

> There has been great sale and Utterance of Wine,
> Besides Beer, Ale and Hippocrass fine,
> In every Country, Region and Nation,
> Chiefly at Billingsgate, at the Salutation;
> And Boreshead near London Stone,
> The Swan at Dowgate, a tavern well Knowne;
> The Mitre in Cheap, and the Bullhead,
> And many like places that make noses red;
> The Boreshead in Old Fish Street, Three Cranes in the Vintree,
> And now of late, Saint Martin's in the Sentree;
> The Windmill in Lothbury, the Ship at the Exchange,
> King's Head in New Fish Street, where Roysters do range;
> The Mermaid in Cornhill, Red Lion in the Strand,
> Three Tuns in Newgate Market, in Old Fish Street the Swan.

There is one belonging to the days just previous to Waterloo, among the last ballads written to celebrate the inn and tavern signs:—

THE MAIL COACH GUARD

At each inn on the road I a welcome could find:—
At the Fleece I'd my skin full of ale;
The Two Jolly Brewers were just to my mind,
At the Dolphin I drank like a whale.
Tom Tun at the Hogshead sold pretty good stuff;
They'd capital flipp at the Boar;
And when at the Angel I'd tippled enough,
I went to the Devil for more.
Then I'd always a sweetheart so snug at the Car;
At the Rose I'd a lily so white;
Few planets could equal sweet Nan at the Star,
No eyes ever twinkled so bright.
I've had many a hug at the sign of the Bear,
In the Sun courted morning and noon;
And when night put an end to my happiness there,
I'd a sweet little girl in the Moon.
To sweethearts and ale I at length bid adieu,
Of wedlock to set up the sign,
Hand in Hand the Good Woman I look for in you,
And the Horns I hope ne'er will be mine.
Once guard to the mail, I'm now guard to the fair;
But though my commission's laid down,
Yet while the King's Arms I'm permitted to bear,
Like a Lion I'll fight for the Crown.

From early days innkeepers were compelled to display a sign; there are Acts of Parliament from the days of Richard II to those of Henry VI with definite rulings on the matter, and the withdrawal of a licence implied the taking away of the sign. Harrison's comments on the expense and elaboration of signs are given on p. 72. During the Great Fire the majority of old London signs were swept away. The surveyors at this period, when the city was rebuilding, seem to have countenanced new projecting signs of enormous size, but later a new Act was passed ordering "in all the streets no signboard should hang across, but that the sign be fixed against the balcony, or some convenient part of the side of the house." Bonnell Thornton, the editor of the *Connoisseur*,

102 THE KING'S ARMS, KENDAL, WESTMORLAND.
An important northern coaching-house

101 THE WHITE BULL, RIBCHESTER, LANCA-
SHIRE. With its Noah's Ark sign and stone
mounting-block

103 THE FIGHTING COCKS, ST ALBANS, HERTFORDSHIRE. A curious
little octagonal building, which, while its claims to great antiquity are probably
exaggerated, may incorporate part of the old Abbey water-gate

in order to burlesque the show of the Society of Artists, got up in the year 1762 a successful Exhibition of Signboards; its catalogue may be read in Larwood and Hotten's *Signboards*. From this time onward legislation seems to have been directed to deter the erection of signs that would be a danger to the public; not only the signboards but the signposts, too, began to be cleared, until by the time Malton was preparing his aquatints the principal streets were comparatively clear. The removing of the posts and the paving of the streets with Scotch granite gave rise to the following epigram:—

> The Scottish new pavement well deserves our praise;
> To the Scotch we're obliged, too, for mending our ways;
> But this we can never forgive, for they say
> As that they have taken our posts all away.

The coach builders and makers of sedan chairs were frequently called upon to paint signboards. It is on record that Cipriani painted a Turk's head, that Samuel Wale, R.A., painted a Falstaff and a full-length Shakespeare. Robert Dalton, keeper of the pictures to George III, served his apprenticeship to a sign- and coach-painter, as well as Ralph Kirby, Thomas Wright of Liverpool, and Smirke the painter. The representation of Admiral Vernon's ship, painted by Peter Monamy, known as the *Portobello*, was well known in the first half of the eighteenth century, and Hogarth's *Man Loaded with Mischief* is one of the most famous of signs painted by a leading artist. Richard Wilson, it is said, painted the *Three Loggerheads* for an inn in North Wales, and from this sign the village of Loggerhead nearby would take its name. This often represents two Loggerheads or fools, the spectator making up the trio.

We now come to George Morland, who knew the roads and inns of the late eighteenth century more thoroughly than the most energetic traveller. He is credited with the *Goat in Boots* that at one time graced an alehouse on the Fulham Road, the *White Lion* for an inn at Paddington, and the sign of *The Cricketers* for a small public-house near Chelsea Bridge. Now we understand Morland's habitual carelessness in money matters it is likely that this artist more than once left a freshly painted sign in lieu of payment for the score. His companion, Julius Caesar Ibbetson, similarly produced a rhyming sign for the village alehouse of Troutbeck in the Lake District. To add to the list we have the names of David Cox, of the elder Crome, of Harlow, Sir Charles Ross, Heming, and lastly Millais, who produced a *St. George and Dragon* with grapes around it for *The Vidlers Inn* at Hayes, Kent.

Lately there has been a revival of activity amongst artists in this connection, due, no doubt, to renewed interest on the part of innkeepers and the public, in spite of the insistence of some big brewing firms on a trade-mark sign of staring monotony. There is, for example, an excellent modern sign at *The Forest Inn*, Hexworthy, representing the inn in miniature. *The Fighting Cocks* (103) and *Postboys* at St. Albans have been repainted by Mr. William Webster Hoare, an amateur artist of advanced age who was once a pupil of Joseph Nash, the topographical draughtsman. Walter Crane contributed the still extant sign of *The Fox and Pelican* at Grayshott, near Hindhead; G. D. Leslie, R.A., painted the sign of *The George and Dragon* at Wargrave on Thames, J. E. Hodgson, R.A., producing the other side showing the saint emptying a well-earned tankard beside the slain dragon, and Mr. F. H. Newberry of the Glasgow School of Art has produced several examples in Dorset. Among other well-known artists is Mr. Ralph Ellis, son of a Sussex naturalist and sign-painter, who studied at the Slade School and in Paris. Recent examples of his varied but always appropriate work include *The Plough and Sail* at Lyminster, *The Royal Oak* at Knockholt, *The Mytton and Mermaid* at Atcham, near Shrewsbury, and the portrait sign of John Nyren at *The Bat and Ball*, Broad Halfpenny Down, with its memories of early cricket. Signs painted by Mr. E. M. Dinkel of the Royal College of Art are to be found at Carlisle, and the work of Mr. H. G. Theaker, of the Polytechnic School of Art, may be seen at Cherry Hinton and Newmarket.

104 THE GREAT WHITE HORSE, IPSWICH. The entrance. Dickens
mentions 'the stone statue of some rampacious animal, with flying
mane and tail, distantly resembling an insane carthorse, which
is elevated above the principal door.'

105 THE KING'S HEAD, CHIGWELL, ESSEX. This great Elizabethan inn is the original of *The Maypole* in Dickens' *Barnaby Rudge*

V

THE INN IN LITERATURE

It is fitting that this chapter, which is in itself in
the nature of a literary pilgrimage, should begin, with
Chaucer's pilgrims of *The Canterbury Tales*, in the yard
of *The Tabard* at Southwark.

> Byfel that, in that seson on a day,
> In Southwerk at the Tabbard as I lay,
> Redy to wenden on my pilgrimage
> To Canturbury with ful devout corage,
> At night was come into that hostelrie
> Wel nyne and twentye in a companye,
> Of sondry folk, by aventure i-falle
> In felowshipe and pilgryms were they alle,
> That toward Canturbury wolden ryde.
> The chambres and the stables weren wyde,
> And wel we weren lodged at the beste.
> And shortly, when the sonne was to reste,
> So hadde I spoken with them everyone,
> That I was of their felowship anon. . . .

The Tabard was one of the largest and stateliest of the
inns of medieval London, and would only have been
used by people of some substance. Its orderly comfort
would have contrasted with the bibulous festivity of the
hedgeside alehouses frequented by working-men and
country people, such as that pictured by Langland in
Piers Plowman, which we quote, as in the case of *The
Canterbury Tales*, from Mr. Burrell's simplified version.
Gluttony, on his way to church, has been tempted into the
village alehouse. . . .

> Then in goes Glutton   and great oaths welcomed him.
> Cis the shoemaker   sat on the bench
> Watt the gamekeeper   and his wife—drunk;
> Tom the tinker   and two of his 'prentices,
> Hick the hackneyman,   Hogg the needler,
> Clarice of Cock Lane,   and the parish clerk;
> Parson Piers of Pray-to-God,   and Pernel the Flemish Woman,
> Daw the ditcher,   and a dozen more of them;
> A fiddler, a ratter,   and a Cheapside scavenger,

67   M

A ropemaker, a trooper,   and Rose of the Small Shop,
A watchman and a hermit,   and the Tyburn hangman;
Godfrey the garlic-seller,   Griffin the Welshman,
All early in the morning   welcomed Glutton gladly
To try the new good ale.

Then cobbler Clement   threw down his cloak,
And said it was for sale   at the New Fair Change.
Hick the hackneyman   threw down his hood,
And bad Bet the butcher   be speaker on his side;
Two then were chosen   the exchange to value—
He that had the goods   should have somewhat with it—
The two rose readily,   and whispered together,
And went aside,   and valued the goods,
They could not in their conscience   truly agree;
Till Robin the ropemaker   was bidden to arise,
And named an umpire   that quarrel should be none.
Hick the ostler   took the cloak,
And Clement took Hick's hood   and a cup of ale,
And held him satisfied;   for if one should repent of it
Sir Glutton should be treated   to a gallon of ale.

There was laughing and chattering   and "Pass the cup round,"
Bargains and toasts and songs,   and so they sat till evensong,
And Glutton had gulped down   a gallon and a gill.

He could neither step nor stand   till he had his staff,
Then he gan to walk   like a blind singer's dog,
Now to this side now to that   and sometimes backward,
Like a man who lays lines   to catch wild birds;
And when he drew to the doorstep   then his eyes grew dim,
He stumbled on the threshold   and fell flat on the floor,
Then Cobbler Clement   caught him by the waist
To lift him up on high   and get him to his knees;
But Glutton was a heavy churl   and groaned as he lifted him,
And coughed up his drink   in Clement's lap.

With all the trouble in the world   his wife and his wench
Bore him home to his bed   and laid him there;
And after all this surfeit   he had a sleeping fit;
All Saturday and Sunday slept   till the sun went to rest.
Then waked he up from his winking   and wiped his eyes,
And the first word he threw was,   "Where's the tankard?" . . .

Other moralists besides Langland liked to castigate the
tipsy joviality of the alehouses. Thus the anonymous
author of *Jacob's Well*, which we quote from the Early
English Text Society's reprint of 1900:—

The other day, I tolde you of the wose of glotony in fyve fote of brede, now schal I telle you where this wose of glotonye begynneth and waxit. At the taverne often the glotonye begynneth. For the taverne is a welle of glotonye, for it may be clepyd the develys scolehous and the develys chapel, for there his dyscyples stodyen and syngyn, bothe day and nighte, and there the devyl doth meraclys to his servauntys. God, in his chapel of holy cherche, makythe blynde men to se, crokyd to go, dombe to speke, deefe to here, and to have alle here righte wyttes; but the feend, in his chapel of the taverne, schewythe his myraclys. He takyth awey mannys feet, that he may noght go, and his tonge, that he may noght speke, alle his wyttes and his bodyly strengthe, this myraclys doth the feend in the taverne.

Now here ye what lesoun he techyth his clerkys in the scole of the taverne. He techyth him glotonye, leccherye, forsweryng, slaundryng, bakbyting, to scorne, to chide, to dyspyse, to reneye God, to stele, to robbe, to fyghte, to sle, and manye othere swiche synnes. And thus he heldyth hem be the throte of glotonye in the scolehous of his taverne. He techyth his dyscyples to mysgoverne there tungys.

But the taverners and their clients persisted in their ungodly ways notwithstanding the denunciations of pietists. The drinking songs of the fifteenth century, despite the pessimism of the age, have a jovial ring, as, for example, this "Song of the Taverner," from the play of Mary Magdalene in *The Digby Plays* (Early English Text Society, 1896):—

> I am a taverner, wytty and wyse,
> That wynys have to sell gret plente.
> Of all the taverners I bere the pryse
> That be dwellyng with-inne the cete;
> Of wynys I havve grete plente,
> Both whyte wynne and red that ys so cleyr:
> Here ys wynne of mawt and Malmeseyn,
> Clary wynne and claret, and other moo,
> Wyn of Gyldyr and of Galles, that made at the grome,
> Wyn of Wyan and Vernage, I seye also;
> Ther be no better, as ferre as ye can goo.

> .   .   .

> Here, lady, is wyn, a repast
> To man, and woman a good restoratyff;
> Ye shall not thynk your mony spent in wast
> From stodyys and hevynes it woll you relyff.

Another favourite theme, that makes its appearance in several versions, is that of the group of jolly wives escaping from their husbands for a surreptitious weekly meeting in a tavern, to which each brings a substantial contribution of food (Wright's *Songs and Carols*, published by the Percy Society):—

> Good gossip mine, where have ye be?
> It is so long sith I you see.
> Where is the best wine? Tell you me.
>   Can you ought tell, (then say) full well.
>
> I know a draught of merry-go-down,
> The best it is in all this town;
> But yet would I not, for my gown,
>   My husband it wist, ye may me trist!
>
> Call forth your gossips by and by,
> Elinor, Joan and Margery,
> Margaret, Alice and Cecily;
>   For they will come both all and some.
>
> And each of them will somewhat bring,
> Goose, pigeon, or capon's wing,
> Pasties of pigeons, or some other thing;
>   For a gallon of wine they will not wring.
>
> Go before by twain and twain,
> Wisely, that ye be not seen;
> For I must home, and come again,
>   To wit ywis where my husband is.
>
> A stripe or two God might send me,
> If my husband might here see me.
> She that is afeared, let her flee.
>   Quoth Alice then: I dread no man.
>
> Now we be in tavern set,
> A draught of the best let him go fet,
> To bring our husbands out of debt;
>   For we will spend, till God more send.
>
> Each of them brought forth their dish
> Some brought flesh, and some (brought) fish.
> Quoth Margaret meek, now with a wish,
>   I would Anne were here, she would make us
>   good cheer.

105 (A) THE WHITE SWAN, STRATFORD-ON-AVON. Elizabethan Wall
Paintings (*circa* 1555) of incidents in the Apocryphal story of Tobit

> How say you, gossips, is this wine good?
> That it is, quoth Elinor, by the rood;
> It cherisheth the heart, and comforteth the blood;
>   Such junkets among shall make us live long. . . .

But then, as now, the practised man-about-town was on his guard against the evil effects of over-indulgence. Here is Thomas Hoccleve, a clerk in the office of the Privy Seal, who wrote a long autobiographical poem under the title of *La Male Règle*:—

> The outward signe of Bachus and his lure,
> That at his dore hangith day by day,
> Excitith (us) to taste of his moisture
> So often, that man can nat wel seyn 'nay.'
> For me, I seye I was enclyned ay
> Withouten daunger thithir for to hye me,
> But if swich charge up on my backe lay
> That I moot it forbere, as for a tyme.

>   .   .   .

> Of him that hauntith taverne of custume,
> At shorte wordes, the profyt is this:
> In double wyse his bagge it shal consume,
> And make his tonge speke of folk amis;
> For in the cuppe seelden founden is,
> That any wight his neigheburgh commendith.
> Behold and see what avantage is his,
> That god, his freend, and eek himselfe, offendith. . . .

As has been seen in a previous chapter, the century that followed the Battle of Bosworth witnessed a nation-wide revival in prosperity under the secure rule of the Tudors. This is reflected in the development of the large inn, as we see it sketched by Harrison in 1583 in his *Description of England*:—

> Those towns that we call thorowfaires have great and sumptuous innes builded in them for the receiving of such travellers and strangers as passe to and fro. The manner of harbouring wherein, is not like that of some other countries, in which the host or goodman of the house dooth chalenge a lordlie authoritie over his ghests, but cleane otherwise, sith everie man may use his inne as his owne house in England, and have for his monie how great or how little varietie of vittels, and what other service himself shall thinke expedient to call for. Our innes are also verie well furnished with naperie:

bedding and tapisterie, especiallie with naperie: for beside the
linnen used at the tables, which is commonlie washed dailie,
is such and so much that belongeth unto the estate and calling
of the ghest. Each commer is sure to lie in cleane sheetes,
wherein no man hath beene lodged since they came from the
landresse. . . . If the traveller hath an horse, his bed dooth
cost him nothing, but if he goe on foot he is sure to paie a
penie for the same: but whether he be horseman or footman,
if his chamber be once appointed, he may carie the kaie with
him, as of his owne house so long as he lodgeth there. If he
loose oughts whilest he abideth in the inne, the host is bound
by a generall custome to restore the damage, so that there is
no greater securitie anie where for travellers than in the gretest
inns of England. Their horses in like sort are walked, dressed
and looked unto by certeine hostelers or hired servants,
appointed at the charges of the goodman of the house, who
in hope of extraordinarie reward will deale verie diligentlie
after outward appearance in this their function and calling.
Herein nevertheless are many of them blameworthie in that
they doo . . . deceive the beast oftentimes of his allowance by
sundrie meanes. . . . It is a world to see how ech owner of
them contendeth with other for goodnesse of interteinement
of their ghests, as about finesse and change of linnen, furniture
of bedding, beautie of roomes, service at the table, costlinesse
of plate, strengthe of drinke, varietie of wines, or well using
of horsses. Finallie there is not so much omitted among them
as the gorgeousness of their verie signes at their doores,
wherein some doo consume thirtie or fortie pounds, a meere
vanitie in mine opinion, but so vaine they will needs be, and
that not onelie to give some outward token of the inne keepers
welth, but also to procure good ghests to the frequenting of
their houses in hope there to be well used.

Nevertheless, there was a darker side to the picture. As
has been seen, throughout the seventeenth century,
ostlers, chamberlains, and even landlords were often
suspected, with some justification, of acting as 'intelligence officers' for highway robbers, and Harrison has
a severe word to say in this connection:—

Certes, I beleeve not that chapman or traveller in England is
robbed by the waie without the knowledge of some of them:
for when he commeth into the inne, and alighteth from his
horsse, the hostler forthwith is verie busie to take down his
budget or capcase in the yard from his sadle bow, which he
peiseth slilie in his hand to feele the weight thereof: or if he
misse of this pitch, when the ghest hath taken up his chamber,

the chamberleine that looketh to the making of the beds, will be sure to remove it from the place where the owner hath set it, as if it were to set it more convenientlie some where else, whereby he getteth an inkling whether it be monie or other short wares, and thereof giveth warning to such od ghests as haunt the house and are of his confederacie, to the utter undoing of manie an honest yeoman as he journeth by the waie. The tapster in like sort for his part dooth mark his behaviour, and what plentie of monie he draweth when he paieth the shot, to the like end: so that it shall be an hard matter to escape all their subtile practises. . . . Some think it a gay matter at their comming to commit their budgets to the goodman of the house: but thereby they oft bewraie themselves. For albeit monie be safe for the time that it is in his hands (for you shall not heare that a man is robbed in his inne) yet after their departure the host can make no warrantise of the same, sith his protection extendeth no further than the gate of his owne house: and there cannot be a surer token unto such as prie and watch for those booties, than to see anie ghest deliver his capcase in such a maner.

The works of the Elizabethan dramatists provide some extraordinarily intimate glimpses into inn and tavern life, reproducing something of the genuine crackle of taproom conversation at this period—we should call it wisecracking nowadays. Here, for example, is a passage from Thomas Middleton's *A Trick to Catch the Old One*:—

A TAVERN

Drawer. You're very welcome, gentlemen.—Dick, show the gentlemen to the Pomegranate then.

Hoard. Hist!

Drawer. Up these stairs, gentlemen.

Hoard. Hist! Drawer!

Drawer. Anon, sir.

Hoard. Prithee, ask at the bar if a gentleman came not in lately? Speak you ay, speak you no?

(*Within*). None came in yet, but Mistress Florence.

Drawer. He says none came in yet, sir, but one Mistress Florence.

Hoard. What is that Florence? A widow?

Drawer. Yes, a Dutch widow.

Hoard. How?

Drawer. That's an English drab, sir; give your worship good morrow.

A not very delicate scene from Beaumont and Fletcher's
The Captain reveals the characteristic nomenclature of the
tavern rooms at this period:—

A ROOM IN A TAVERN

Boy. Score a gallon of sack, and a pint of Olives, to the Unicorn.
Above within. Why, drawer.
Boy. Anon! Anon!
Another Boy. Look into the Nags-head there.
2nd Boy. Score a quart of claret to the Bar. And a pound of
    sausages into the Flower-pot.
    Enter first servant with wine.
1st Servant. The devil's in their throats, Anon, Anon!
    Enter second servant.
2nd Servant. Mull a pint of sack there for the women in the
    Flower-de-Luce, and put in ginger enough; they belch
    like pot-guns; and, Robin, fetch tobacco for the Peacock.

This system of giving each room an individual name
was universal, and there is a delightfully intimate touch
in Hostess Quickly's reproach to Falstaff in Shakespeare's
Henry IV:—

Falstaff. Why, what do I owe thee, then?
Hostess. Marry, if thou wert an honest man, thyself and the
    money too. Thou didst swear to me upon a parcel-gilt
    goblet, sitting in my Dolphin-chamber, at the round
    table, by a sea-coal fire, on Wednesday in Whitsun-week,
    when the prince broke thy head for liking his father to a
    singing-man of Windsor; thou didst swear to me then,
    as I was washing thy wound, to marry me, and make
    me my lady thy wife.

In the same play we get a glimpse of the rough-
and-ready accommodation still provided for labouring
travellers in the famous inn-yard scene at Rochester:—

2nd Carrier. I think this is the most villainous house in all
    London road for fleas: I am stung like a tench.
1st Carrier. Like a tench? By the mass, there is ne'er a king in
    Christendom could be better bit than I have been since
    the first cock.
2nd Carrier. Why, you will allow us ne'er a jordan, and then we
    leak in your chimney; and your chamberlie breeds fleas
    like a loach.
1st Carrier. What, ostler! Come away, and be hanged, come
    away.

The same contrast between the well-appointed comfortable hostelry and the wretched hovel of remote places continued into the seventeenth century. The reliable Fynes Moryson, in about 1625, claims that "the world affoords not such Innes as England hath"—a remark of double-edged interpretation. His picture is of free-handed hospitality, though like Harrison he has a word to say on the ostlers' dodges. Here he describes the arrival of a traveller at a typical English inn:—

Another servant gives the passenger his private chamber, and kindles his fier, the third puls of his bootes, and makes them cleane. Then the Host or Hostesse visit him, and if he will eate with the Host, or at a common Table with others, his meale will cost him sixe pence, or in some places foure pence (yet this course is lesse honourable, and not used by Gentlemen): but if he will eate in his chamber, he commands what meate he will according to his appetite, and as much as thinkes fit for him and his company, yea, the kitchen is open to him, to command the meate to be dressed as he best likes; and when he sits at Table, the Host or Hostesse will accompany him, or if they have many Guests, will at least visit him, taking it curtesie to be bid to sit downe: while he eates, if he have companie especiallie, he shall be offred musicke, which he may freely take or refuse, and if he be solitary, the Musitians will give himm the good day with musicke in the morning. It is the custome, and no way disgracefull, to set up part of supper for his breakfast: in the evening or in the morning after breakfast, (for the common sort use not to dine, but ride from breakfast to supper time, yet comming early to the Inne, for better resting of their Horses) he shall have a reckoning in writing, and if it seeme unreasonable, the Host will satisfie him, either for the due price, or by abating part, especially if the servant deceive him in any way, which one of experience will soone find.

Against this may be set the nightmare experience of John Taylor, the 'Water Poet,' in 1649, who, having torn his breeches on a stile and got them roughly patched at Bridgwater, "came to a ragged market town called Neatherstoy" (Nether Stowey, under the Quantocks), where:—

I took up my lodging at a sign and no sign, which formerly was The Rose and Crown, but Roses are withered and Crowns

George Inn. But we have written enough of the seamier side of seventeenth-century travel. Before we leave this period, we must add a paragraph from Izaak Walton's *Compleat Angler*, to show that there were some country alehouses at least where the wayfarer was certain of a warm welcome and good cleanly comfort. Thus *The Thatched House* at Hoddesdon:—

> *Piscator to Venator:* I am glad your patience hath held out so long, for we are in sight of the Thatched House. I'll now lead you to an honest Ale-house, where we shall find a cleanly room, lavender in the windows, and twenty ballads stuck about the wall. There my hostess, which I may tell you is both cleanly and handsome, and civil, hath dressed many a fish for me; and shall now dress it after my fashion and I warrant it good meat.

The remarkable increase during the early years of the eighteenth century in the number of London signs, used by tradesmen and innkeepers alike, is apparent in a paper by Addison, published in the *Spectator* for April 2, 1710, which provides a somewhat depreciatory survey of their multifarious names and combinations.

> There is nothing like sound literature and good sense to be met with in those objects, that are everywhere thrusting themselves out to the eye and endeavouring to become visible. Our streets are filled with *blue boars, black swans* and *red lions,* not to mention *flying pigs* and *hogs in armour,* with many creatures more extraordinary than any in the deserts of Africa. Strange that one, who has all the birds and beasts in nature to choose out of, should live at the sign of an *ens rationis.*
>
> My first task, therefore, should be, like that of Hercules, to clear the city from monsters. In the second place, I should forbid that creatures of jarring and incongruous natures should be joined together in the same sign; such as the *Bell and the Neat's Tongue,* and the *Dog and Gridiron.* The *Fox and the Goose* may be supposed to have met, but what has the *Fox and the Seven Stars* to do together? And when did the *Lamb and Dolphin* ever meet but on a signpost? As for the *Cat and Fiddle,* there is a conceit in it, and therefore I do not intend that anything I have here said should affect it. I must, however, observe to you upon this subject, that it is usual for a young tradesman, upon its first setting up, to add to his own sign that of the master whom he served, as the husband, after marriage, gives a place to his mistress' arms in his own coat. This I take to

105 (B) THE WHITE SWAN, STRATFORD-ON-AVON.
Another Elizabethan Wall Painting, recently
disclosed, in the Tobit series

have given rise to many of those absurdities which are committed over our heads; and, as I am informed, first occasioned the *Three Nuns and a Hare*, which we see so frequently joined together. I would therefore establish certain rules for the determining how far one tradesman may give the sign of another, and in what case he may be allowed to quarter it with his own.

In the third place, I would enjoin every shop to make use of a sign which bears some affinity to the wares in which it deals. What can be more inconsistent than to see a bawd at the sign of the *Angel*, or a tailor at the *Lion*. A cook should not live at the *Boot*, nor a shoemaker at the *Roasted Pig*; and yet, for want of this regulation, I have seen a *Goat* set up before the door of a perfumer, and the *French King's Head* at a sword-cutler's.

An ingenious foreigner observes that several of those gentlemen who value themselves upon their families, and overlook such as are bred to trades, bear the tools of their forefathers in their coats-of-arms. I will not examine how true this is in fact; but though it may not be necessary for posterity thus to set up the sign of their forefathers, I think it highly proper that those who actually profess the trade should show some such mark of it before their doors.

When the name gives the occasion for an ingenious signpost, I would likewise advise the owner to take that opportunity of letting the world know who he is. It would have been ridiculous for the ingenious Mrs. Salmon to have lived at the sign of the trout, for which reason she has erected before her house the figure of the fish that is her namesake. Mr. Bell has likewise distinguished himself by a device of the same nature. And here, sir, I must beg leave to observe to you that this particular figure of a bell has given occasion to several pieces of wit in this head. A man of your reading must know that Abel Drugger gained great applause by it in the time of Ben Jonson. Our Apocryphal heathen god is also represented by this figure, which, in conjunction with the Dragon makes a very handsome picture in several of our streets. As for the *Bell Savage*, which is the sign of a savage man standing by a bell, I was formerly very much puzzled upon the conceit of it, till I accidentally fell into the reading of an old romance translated out of the French, which gives an account of a very beautiful woman, who was found in a wilderness, and is called *La Belle Sauvage*, and is everywhere translated by our countrymen *the Bell Savage*.[1] This piece of philology will, I hope, convince you that I have made signposts my study, and consequently qualified myself for the employment which I solicit at your hands. But before I conclude my letter, I must communicate to you another remark

---

[1] Addison is, of course, quite mistaken in his interpretation.

which I have made upon the subject with which I am now entertaining you—namely, that I can give a shrewd guess at the humour of the inhabitant by the sign that hangs before his door. A surly, choleric fellow generally makes choice of a *Bear*, as men of milder dispositions frequently live at the *Lamb*. Seeing a *Punch-bowl* painted upon a sign near Charing Cross, and very curiously garnished, with a couple of angels hovering over it and squeezing a lemon into it, I had the curiosity to ask after the master of the house, and found upon enquiry, as I had guessed by the little *agrémens* upon his sign, that he was a Frenchman.

We have already drawn a bow at a venture, and identified *The Black Lion* of Smollett's *Sir Launcelot Greaves* with the delightful Georgian *White Horse* at Eaton Socon on the Great North Road (24). The opening paragraph of that full-blooded romance is certainly worth quoting here, if only to give some idea of the average reception accorded to the chance wayfarer arriving at any smaller inn of the better type during the mid-eighteenth century:—

It was on the great northern road from York to London, about the beginning of the month of October, and the hour of eight in the evening, that four travellers were, by a violent shower of rain, driven for shelter into a little public-house on the side of the highway, distinguished by a sign which was said to exhibit the sign of a black lion. The kitchen, in which they assembled, was the only room for entertainment in the house, paved with red bricks, remarkably clean, furnished with three or four Windsor chairs, adorned with shining plates of pewter, and copper saucepans, nicely scoured, that even dazzled the eyes of the beholder; while a cheerful fire of sea-coal blazed in the chimney. Three of the travellers, who arrived on horseback, having seen their cattle properly accommodated in the stable, agreed to pass the time, until the weather should clear up, over a bowl of rumbo, which was accordingly prepared. But the fourth, refusing to join their company, took his station on the opposite side of the chimney, and called for a pint of twopenny, with which he indulged himself apart. At a little distance, on his left hand, there was another group, consisting of the landlady, a decent widow, her two daughters, . . . and a country lad who served both as waiter and ostler. . . .

The events that took place at *The Black Lion* are outside the scope of these pages, but its interior is definitely recalled in Goldsmith's graphic little picture of the inn parlour in *The Deserted Village*:—

> Imagination fondly stoops to trace
> The parlour splendours of that festive place;
> The white-washed wall, the nicely sanded floor,
> The varnished clock that clicked behind the door.
> The chest contrived a double debt to pay—
> A bed by night, a chest of drawers by day.
> The pictures placed for ornament and use,
> The twelve good rules, the royal game of goose,
> The hearth, except when winter ruled the day,
> With aspen boughs and flowers of fennel gay,
> While broken tea-cups, wisely kept for show,
> Ranged o'er the chimney glistened in a row.

Towards the close of the century, there is evidence of Dr. Johnson's rich approval of inns in numerous passages reported by Boswell, of which we reproduce a couple.

'There is no private house,' said Johnson, talking on this subject, 'in which people can enjoy themselves so well as at a capital tavern. Let there be ever so great a plenty of good things, ever so much grandeur, ever so much elegance, ever so much desire that everybody should be easy, in the nature of things it cannot be: there must always be some degree of care and anxiety. The master of the house is anxious to entertain his guests; the guests are anxious to be agreeable to him; and no man but a very impudent dog indeed can as freely command what is in another man's house as if it were his own. Whereas, at a tavern, there is a general freedom from anxiety. You are sure you are welcome; and the more noise you make, the more trouble you give, the more good things you call for, the welcomer you are. No servants will attend you with the alacrity which waiters do, who are incited by the prospect of an immediate reward in proportion as they please. No, sir, there is nothing which has yet been contrived by man, by which so much happiness is produced, as by a good tavern or inn.' He then repeated with great emotion Shenstone's lines:—

> 'Whoe'er has travelled life's dull round,
>   Where'er his stages may have been,
> May sigh to think he still has found
>   The warmest welcome at an inn.'

And again:—

In contradiction to those who, having a wife and children, prefer domestic enjoyments to those which a tavern affords, I have heard him (Johnson) assert that *a tavern chair was the throne of human felicity*. As soon (said he) as I enter the door of a tavern, I experience an oblivion of care, and a freedom from solicitude: when I am seated, I find the master courteous, and the servants obsequious to my call, anxious to know and ready to supply my wants: wine there exhilarates my spirits, and prompts me to free conversation, and an interchange of discourse with those whom I most love; I dogmatize, and am contradicted; and in this conflict of opinions and sentiments I find delight.

It is difficult to conceive of the great Doctor being accorded anything but the most obsequious attention at either inn or tavern. But with others it was different; and the German pastor, C. P. Moritz, whose *Travels through Several Parts of England* in the year 1782 were undertaken, rather eccentrically, on foot, with a miniature Milton in his pocket for wayside solace, records how he is—

now confirmed in my suspicions, that, in England, any person undertaking so long a journey on foot, is sure to be looked upon and considered as either a beggar, or a vagabond, or some necessitous wretch, which is a character not much more popular than that of a rogue; so that I could now easily account for my reception in Windsor, and at Nuneham. But, with all my partiality for this country, it is impossible, even in theory, and much less so in practice, to approve of a system that confines all the pleasures and benefits of travel to the rich. A poor peripatetic is hardly allowed the humble merit of being honest.

His experiences at Windsor and Nuneham are worth quoting at length. At the former—

As I entered the inn, and desired to have something to eat, the countenance of the waiter soon gave me to understand that I should there find no very friendly reception. Whatever I got, they seemed to give me, with such an air, as shewed too plainly how little they thought of me; and as if they considered me but as a beggar. I must do them the justice to own, however, that they suffered me to pay like a gentleman. No doubt this was the first time this pert bepowdered puppy had ever been called on to wait on a poor devil, who entered their place on foot. I was tired; and asked for a bedroom, where I might sleep. They showed me into one, that much resembled a prison for malefactors. I requested that I might have a better room at night. On which, without any apology, they told me, that they had no intention of lodging me, as they had no room for such guests; but that I might go back to Slough, where very probably I might get a night's lodging.[1]

At Nuneham, the good pastor was "not a little tired: and it was also quite dark. . . ."

At length, quite at the end of the place, I perceived a great sign hanging across the street, and the last house to the left was the inn, at which every thing seemed to be still in motion.

I entered without ceremony, and told them my errand; which was, that I intended to sleep there that night. "By no means," was the answer, "it was utterly impossible; the whole house was full, and all their beds engaged; and, as I had come so far, I might even as well walk on the remaining five miles to Oxford."

Being very hungry, I requested that, at least, they would give me something to eat. To this they answered, that, as I could not stay all night there, it would be more proper for me to sup where I lodged; and so I might go on.

At length, quite humbled by the untowardness of my circumstances, I asked for a pot of beer, and that they did vouchsafe to give me, for ready money only: but a bit of bread, to eat with it (for which also I would willingly have paid) they peremptorily refused me.

Such unparalleled inhospitality I really could not have expected in an English inn: but, resolving, with a kind of spiteful indignation, to see how far their inhumanity would carry them, I begged that they would only let me sleep on a bench, and merely give me house-room; adding, that if they would grant me that boon only, I would pay them the same as for a bed; for, that I was so tired, I could not possibly go any farther. Even in the moment that I was thus humbly soliciting this humble boon, they banged the door to full in my face.

Moritz draws a very different picture to Hazlitt, whose essay *On Going a Journey*, written in the early years of the nineteenth century, is one of the most delightful things in inn literature.

. . . How fine it is to enter some old town, walled and turreted just at the approach of night-fall, or to come to some straggling village, with the lights streaming through the surrounding

---

[1] Moritz's parting experiences at Windsor are recorded on page 20.

N

gloom; and then after inquiring for the best entertainment that the place affords, to "take one's ease at one's inn!" These eventful moments in our lives' history are too precious, too full of solid, heart-felt happiness to be frittered and dribbled away in imperfect sympathy. I would have them all to myself, and drain them to the last drop: they will do to talk of or to write about afterwards. What a delicate speculation it is, after drinking whole goblets of tea,

> "The cup that cheers, but not inebriates,"

and letting the fumes ascend into the brain, to sit considering what we shall have for supper—eggs and a rasher, a rabbit smothered in onions, or an excellent veal-cutlet! . . . The *incognito* of an inn is one of its striking privileges—"lord of one's-self, uncumber'd with a name." Oh! it is great to shake off the trammels of the world and of public opinion—to lose our importunate, tormenting, everlasting personal identity in the elements of nature, and become the creature of the moment, clear of all ties—to hold to the universe only by a dish of sweet-breads, and to owe nothing but the score of the evening —and no longer seeking for applause and meeting with contempt, to be known by no other title but *the Gentleman in the parlour*.

An incident recorded by Cobbett in his *Rural Rides* at the same time goes to show that not all innkeepers were the churls that Moritz's adventures would lead us to believe:—

I set out from Heytesbury this morning about six o'clock. Last night, before I went to bed, I found that there were some men and boys in the house, who had come all the way from Bradford, about twelve miles, in order to get nuts. These were men and boys that had been employed in the cloth factories at Bradford and about Bradford. I had some talk with some of these nutters, and I am quite convinced, not that the cloth making is at an end, but that it will never be again what it has been. Before last Christmas, these manufacturers had full work, at one shilling and threepence a yard at broad cloth weaving. They have now a quarter work, and one shilling a yard! One and threepence a yard for this weaving has been given at all times within the memory of man! Nothing can show more clearly than this, and in a stronger light, the great change which has taken place in the remuneration of labour. There was a turn-out last winter, when the price was reduced to a shilling a yard; but it was put an end to in the usual way; the constable's staff, the bayonet, the gaol. These poor nutters were extremely ragged. I saved my supper, and I fasted instead of breakfasting. That was three shillings that I had saved, and I added five to them, with a resolution to save them afterwards, in order to give these chaps a breakfast for once in their lives. There were eight of them, six men and two boys; and I gave them two quartern loaves, two pounds of cheese, and eight pints of strong beer. The fellows were very thankful, but the conduct of the landlord and landlady pleased me exceedingly. When I came to pay my bill, they had said nothing about my bed, which had been a very good one; and, when I asked, why they had not put the bed into the bill, they said they would not charge anything for the bed, since I had been so good to the poor men. Yes, said I, but I must now throw the expense upon you. I had no supper, and I have had no breakfast, and, therefore, I am not called upon to pay for them, but I have had the bed. It ended by my paying for the bed, and coming off, leaving the nutters at their breakfast, and very much delighted with the landlord and his wife; and I must here observe that I have pretty generally found a good deal of compassion for the poor people to prevail amongst publicans and their wives.

Likewise Washington Irving, in *Travelling at Christmas*, draws a delightful picture of an evening arrival at an inn.

In the evening we reached a village where I had determined to pass the night. As we drove into the great gateway of the inn, I saw on one side the light of a rousing kitchen fire beaming through a window. I entered, and admired for the hundredth time, that picture of convenience, neatness, and broad honest enjoyment, the kitchen of an English inn. It was of spacious dimensions; hung round by copper and tin vessels, highly polished, and decorated here and there with a Christmas green. Hams, tongues, and flitches of bacon, were suspended from the ceiling; a smoke-jack made its ceaseless clanking beside the fire-place, and a clock ticked in one corner. A well scoured deal table extended along one side of the kitchen, with a cold round of beef, and other hearty viands upon it, over which two foaming tankards of ale seemed mounting guard. Travellers of inferior order were preparing to attack this stout repast, while others sat smoking or gossiping over their ale, on two high-backed oaken settles beside the fire.

Trim housemaids were hurrying backwards and forwards under the directions of a fresh, bustling landlady; but still seizing an occasional moment to exchange a flippant word, and have a rallying laugh with the group round the fire. The scene completely realised poor Robin's humble idea of the comforts of mid-winter:—

'Now trees their leafy hats do bare,
To reverence Winter's silver hair;
A handsome hostess, merry host,
A pot of ale now and a toast,
Tobacco and a good coal fire,
Are things this season doth require.'

As has been seen, the first quarter of the nineteenth
century saw the culmination of coach travel and inn
prosperity in this country. No chapter on these lines
would be complete without some account of a journey in
the old style, with its intimate sidelights on inn life; so
here we give a part (we would like to give the whole) of
that very exciting chapter in *Tom Brown's School-days* in
which the hero makes his first trip to Rugby by stage
coach in the reign of King William IV.

"Now, sir, time to get up, if you please. Tally-ho coach for
Leicester'll be round in half an hour, and don't wait for
nobody." So spake the boots of the Peacock Inn, Islington,
at half-past two o'clock on the morning of a day in the early
part of November 183–, giving Tom at the same time a shake
by the shoulder, and then putting down a candle and carrying
off his shoes to clean.

Tom and his father arrived in town from Berkshire the
day before, and finding, on inquiry, that the Birmingham
coaches that ran from the city did not pass through Rugby,
but deposited their passengers at Dunchurch, a village three
miles distant on the main road, where said passengers had to
wait for the Oxford and Leicester coach in the evening, or to
take a post-chaise, had resolved that Tom should travel down
by the Tally-ho, which diverged from the main road and passed
through Rugby itself. And as the Tally-ho was an early coach,
they had driven out to the Peacock to be on the road.

Tom had never been in London, and would have liked to
have stopped at the Belle Savage, where they had been put
down by the Star, just at dusk, that he might have gone roving
about those endless, mysterious, gas-lit streets, which, with
their glare, and hum, and moving crowds, excited him so that
he couldn't talk even. But as soon as he found that the Peacock
arrangement would get him to Rugby by twelve o'clock in
the day, whereas otherwise he wouldn't be there till the evening,
all other plans melted away, his one absorbing aim being to
become a public-school boy as fast as possible, and six hours
sooner or later seeming to him of the most alarming importance.

Tom and his father had alighted at the Peacock at about

seven in the evening; and having heard with unfeigned joy the paternal order, at the bar, of steaks and oyster-sauce for supper in half an hour, and seen his father seated cozily by the bright fire in the coffee-room with the paper in his hand, Tom had run out to see about him, had wondered at all the vehicles passing and repassing, and had fraternized with the boots and hostler, from whom he ascertained that the Tally-ho was a tip-top goer—ten miles an hour including stoppages—and so punctual that all the road set their clocks by her.

Then being summoned to supper, he had regaled himself in one of the bright little boxes of the Peacock coffee-room, on the beef-steak and unlimited oyster-sauce and brown stout (tasted then for the first time—a day to be marked for ever by Tom with a white stone); had at first attended to the excellent advice which his father was bestowing on him from over his glass of steaming brandy-and-water, and then began nodding, from the united effects of the stout, the fire, and the lecture; till the Squire, observing Tom's state, and remembering that it was nearly nine o'clock, and that the Tally-ho left at three, sent the little fellow off to the chambermaid, with a shake of the hand (Tom having stipulated in the morning before starting that kissing should now cease between them), and a few parting words. . . .

. . . At ten minutes to three he was down in the coffee-room in his stockings, carrying his hat-box, coat, and comforter in his hand; and there he found his father nursing a bright fire, and a cup of hot coffee and a hard biscuit on the table.

"Now then, Tom, give us your things here, and drink this. There's nothing like starting warm, old fellow."

Tom addressed himself to the coffee, and prattled away while he worked himself into his shoes and his great-coat, well warmed through—a Petersham coat with velvet collar, made tight after the abominable fashion of those days. And just as he is swallowing his last mouthful, winding his comforter round his throat, and tucking the ends into the breast of his coat, the horn sounds; boots looks in and says, "Tally-ho, sir"; and they hear the ring and the rattle of the four fast trotters and the town-made drag, as it dashes up to the Peacock.

"Anything for us, Bob?" says the burly guard, dropping down from behind, and slapping himself across the chest.

"Young gen'lm'n, Rugby; three parcels, Leicester; hamper o' game, Rugby," answers hostler.

"Tell young gent to look alive," says the guard, opening the hind-boot and shooting in the parcels, after examining them by the lamps. "Here, shove the portmanteau up a-top. I'll fasten him presently.—Now then, sir, jump up behind."

face is about the colour of the tails of his old pink, as he exchanges greetings with coachman and guard. Now they pull up at a lodge, and take on board a well muffled-up sportsman, with his gun-case and carpet-bag. An early up-coach meets them, and the coachmen gather up their horses, and pass one another with the accustomed lift of the elbow, each team doing eleven miles an hour, with a mile to spare behind if necessary. And here comes breakfast.

"Twenty minutes here, gentlemen," says the coachman, as they pull up at half-past seven at the inn door.

Have we not endured nobly this morning? and is not this a worthy reward for much endurance? There is the low, dark wainscoted room hung with sporting prints; the hat-stand (with a whip or two standing up in it belonging to bagmen who are still snug in bed) by the door; the blazing fire, with the quaint old glass over the mantelpiece, in which is stuck a large card, with the list of the meets for the week of the county hounds; the table, covered with the whitest of cloths and of china, and bearing a pigeon pie, ham, round of cold boiled beef cut from a mammoth ox, and the great loaf of household bread on a wooden trencher. And here comes in the stout head waiter, puffing under a tray of hot viands—kidneys and a steak, transparent rashers and poached eggs, buttered toast and muffins, coffee and tea, all smoking hot. The table can never hold it all. The cold meats are removed to the sideboard—they were only put on for show and to give us an appetite. And now, fall on, gentlemen all. It is a well-known sporting house, and the breakfasts are famous. Two or three men in pink, on their way to the meet, drop in, and are very jovial and sharp-set, as indeed we all are.

"Tea or coffee, sir?" says the head waiter coming round to Tom.

"Coffee please," says Tom, with his mouth full of muffin and kidney. Coffee is a treat to him, tea is not.

Our coachman, I perceive, who breakfasts with us, is a cold beef man. He also eschews hot potations, and addicts himself to a tankard of ale, which is brought him by the barmaid. Sportsman looks on approvingly, and orders a ditto for himself.

Tom has eaten kidney and pigeon pie, and imbibed coffee, till his little skin is as tight as a drum; and then has the further pleasure of paying head waiter out of his own purse, in a dignified manner, and walks out before the inn door to see the horses put to. This is done leisurely and in a highly finished manner by the hostlers, as if they enjoyed the not being hurried. Coachman comes out with his waybill, and puffing a fat cigar which the sportsman has given him. Guard emerges from the tap, where he prefers breakfasting, licking round a tough-looking doubtful cheroot, which you might tie round your finger, and three whiffs of which would knock any one else out of time.

The pinks stand about the inn door, lighting cigars and waiting to see us start, while their hacks are led up and down the market-place, on which the inn looks. They all know our sportsman, and we feel a reflected credit when we see him chatting and laughing with them.

"Now, sir, please," says the coachman. All the rest of the passengers are up; the guard is locking up the hind boot.

"A good run to you," says the sportsman to the pinks, and is by the coachman's side in no time.

"Let 'em go, Dick!" The hostlers fly back, drawing off the cloths from their glossy loins, and away we go, through the market-place and down the High Street, looking in at the first-floor windows, and seeing several worthy burgesses shaving thereat; while all the shop-boys who are cleaning the windows, and housemaids who are doing the steps, stop and look pleased as we rattle past, as if we were a part of their legitimate morning's amusement. We clear the town, and are well out between the hedgerows again as the town clock strikes eight. . . .

Pickwick appeared in 1837, the year of Queen Victoria's accession, when the inns were still enjoying their heyday. Its packed pages contain some delightful thumbnail sketches of famous houses, of which we select a few almost at random. Here, for example, is *The Great White Horse* at Ipswich, illustrated in these pages (43, 104):—

In the main street of Ipswich, on the left-hand side of the way, a short distance after you have passed through the open space fronting the town-hall, stands an inn known far and wide by the appellation of the Great White Horse, rendered the more conspicuous by a stone statue of some rampacious animal with flowing mane and tail, distantly resembling an insane cart-horse, which is elevated above the principal door. The Great White Horse is famous in the neighbourhood, in the same degree as a prize ox, or a county-paper-chronicled turnip, or unwieldy pig—for its enormous size. Never was such labyrinths of uncarpeted passages, such clusters of mouldy ill-lighted rooms, such huge number of small dens for eating or sleeping in, beneath any one roof, as are collected together between the four walls of the Great White Horse at Ipswich.[1]

---

[1] Were he alive to-day, Dickens would certainly revise his opinion of this well-run establishment.

And here is a typical London public-house, *The Magpie and Stump*, "happy in the double advantage of being in the vicinity of Clare Market, and closely approximating to the back of New Inn":—

This favoured tavern, sacred to the evening orgies of Mr. Lowten and his companions, was what ordinary people would designate a public-house. That the landlord was a man of money-making turn was sufficiently testified by the fact of a small bulkhead beneath the tap-room window, in size and shape not unlike a sedan-chair, being underlet to a mender of shoes: and that he was a being of philanthropic mind was evident from the protection he afforded to a pieman, who vended his delicacies without fear of interruption, on the very door-step. In the lower windows, which were decorated with curtains of a saffron hue, dangled two or three printed cards bearing reference to Devonshire cider and Dantzig spruce, while a large blackboard, announcing in white letters to an enlightened public, that there were 500,000 barrels of double stout in the cellars of the establishment, left the mind in a not unpleasing state of doubt and uncertainty as to the precise direction in the bowels of the earth, in which this mighty cavern might be supposed to extend. When we add that the weather-beaten signboard bore the half-obliterated semblance of a magpie intently eyeing a crooked streak of brown paint, which the neighbours had been taught from infancy to consider as the "stump," we have said all that need be said of the exterior of the edifice.

The Marquis of Granby, at Dorking, "was quite the model of a roadside public-house of the better class—just large enough to be convenient, and small enough to be snug. . . ."

On the opposite side of the road was a large sign-board on a high post, representing the head and shoulders of a gentleman with an apoplectic countenance, in a red coat with deep blue facings, and a touch of the same blue over his three-cornered hat for a sky. Over that again were a pair of flags; beneath the last button of his coat were a pair of cannon; and the whole formed an expressive and undoubted likeness of the Marquis of Granby, of glorious memory.

The bar window displayed a choice collection of geranium plants, and a well-dusted row of spirit phials. The open shutters bore a variety of golden inscriptions, eulogistic of good beds and neat wines; and the choice group of countrymen and hostlers lounging about the stable door and horse-trough, afforded presumptive proof of the excellent quality of the ale and spirits which were sold within.

The Commercial Room of *The Peacock* at "Eatanswill"

differed in no material respect from the generality of such apartments; that is to say, it was a large, bare-looking room the furniture of which had no doubt been better had it been newer, with a spacious table in the centre, and a variety of smaller dittos in the corners; an extensive assortment of variously shaped chairs, and an old Turkey carpet, bearing about the same relative importance to the size of the room, as a lady's pocket-handkerchief might to the floor of a watch-box. The walls were garnished with one or two large maps; and several weather-beaten rough greatcoats, with complicated capes, dangled from a long row of pegs in one corner. The mantel-shelf was ornamented with a wooden inkstand, containing one stump of a pen and half a wafer; a road-book and a directory; a county history minus the cover; and the mortal remains of a trout in a glass coffin. The atmosphere was redolent of tobacco-smoke, the fumes of which had communicated a rather dingy hue to the whole room, and more especially to the dusty red curtains which shaded the windows. On the sideboard a variety of miscellaneous articles were huddled together, the most conspicuous of which were some very cloudy fish-sauce cruets, a couple of driving-boxes, two or three whips, and as many travelling shawls, a tray of knives and forks, and the mustard.

Finally we have the Travellers' Room at *The White Horse Cellar* in Piccadilly, the great coaching terminus near the site of the present Berkeley Hotel, whose appearance is preserved for us in a delightful colour print by Pollard.

The travellers' room of the White Horse Cellar is of course uncomfortable; it would be no travellers' room if it were not. It is the right-hand parlour, into which an aspiring kitchen-fireplace appears to have walked, accompanied by a rebellious poker, tongs and shovel. It is divided into boxes, for the solitary confinement of travellers, and is furnished with a clock, a looking-glass, and a live waiter, which latter article is kept in a small kennel for washing glasses, in a corner of the apartment.

Another famous Dickens's inn was *The King's Head* at Chigwell (105), which, from its Tudor associations, the novelist, in *Barnaby Rudge*, renamed *The Maypole*.

The Maypole was an old building with more gable ends than a lazy man would care to count on a sunny day; huge zigzag chimneys, out of which it seemed that even smoke could not choose to come in more than naturally fantastic shapes, imparted to it in its tortuous progress; and vast stables, gloomy, ruinous and empty. The place was said to have been built in the days of King Henry VIII, and there was a legend that Queen Elizabeth had not only slept there one night while on a hunting excursion, in a certain oak-panelled room with a deep bay-window, but that next morning, while standing on a mounting-block before the door, with one foot in the stirrup, the Virgin monarch had then and there boxed and cuffed an unlucky page for some neglect of duty.

With its overhanging stories, drowsy little panes of glass, and front bulging out and projecting over the pathway, the old house looked as if it were nodding in its sleep. Indeed it needed no great stretch of fancy to detect in it other re-semblances to humanity. The bricks of which it was built had originally been a deep, dark red, but had grown yellow and discoloured like an old man's skin; the sturdy timbers had decayed like teeth, and here and there the ivy, like a warm garment to comfort it in its age, wrapt its green leaves closely round the time-worn walls.

The solid comfort and plentiful fare that the greater houses offered at this period impressed even the fastidious Disraeli. There is a passage in *Tancred* that can still make our mouths water:—

"The coach stops here half an hour, gentlemen: dinner quite ready."

'Tis a delightful sound. And what a dinner! What a pro-fusion of substantial delicacies! What mighty and iris-tinted rounds of beef! What vast and marble-veined ribs! What gelatinous veal pies! What colossal hams! Those are evidently prize cheeses! And how invigorating is the perfume of those various and variegated pickles! Then the bustle emulating the plenty; the ringing of bells, the clash of thoroughfare, the summoning of ubiquitous waiters, and the all-pervading feeling of omnipotence from the guests, who order what they please to the landlord, who can produce and execute everything they can desire. 'Tis a wondrous sight!

Even after the coming of the railways, when the stage coaches were little more than a memory on the roads, and a somnolence had fallen on the great yards, local festivities and celebrations could, if only for a few days, bring back something of the old clatter and bustle. Such an occasion was the famous Hunt Dinner and Ball at *Handley Cross*.

At an early hour in the afternoon numerous rural vehicles came jingling into Handley Cross, with the mud of many counties on their wheels. There was such a ringing of bells, calling of waiters, cursing of chamber-maids, and blasting of boots, at the various hotels, in consequence of the inability of the houses to swell themselves into three times their size, to accommodate the extraordinary influx of guests. "Very sorry indeed," says Mr. Snubbins, the landlord of the Dragon, twisting a dirty duster round his thumb, "very sorry indeed, sir," speaking to a red-faced, big-whiskered head, thrust out of a carriage window, "we are full to the attics—not a shake-down or sofa unoccupied; can get you a nice lodging out if you like—very comfortable."

"D—— your comfortables, you lying thief!—do you suppose I can't do that for myself? Well, if ever you catch me coming to your house again I hope I may be ——." The wish was lost by some one pulling the irate gentleman back into his chaise, and after a short parley inside, during which three reasonable single gentlemen applied to Mr. Snubbins for the accommodation of a room amongst them to dress in for dinner, the boy was ordered to drive on, and make the grand tour of the inns.

Weary, most weary were the doings at the Dragon. *Ring a ding, ding a ding dong*, went the hostler's bell at the gate; "Room for a carriage and pair?"

"Whose o' it?"

"Mrs. Grout's!"

"No, quite full!" The hostler muttering to himself, "Mrs. Grout's and two feeds—sixpence for hostler." *Ring a ding, ding a ding, ding a ding dong.* Hostler again—"Coming out!" "Who now?" "Squire Gooseander! four posters, piping hot, white lather, boys beery, four on to Hollinshall, bait there, back to hall—sixpence a mile for good driving—out they come—there's your ticket—pay back and away."

Tinkle, tinkle, tinkle, tinkle, tinkle, tinkle, tinkle, went a little bell, as though it would never stop.

"WAITER!" roared a voice from the top of the house, that came like a crash of thunder after the insignificant precursor, "am I to ring here all day? Where's the boots? I sent him for a barber an hour ago, and here I've been starving in my shirt-sleeves ever since."

"Now, Jane, Miss Tramp wants her shoes."

"Where's the chambermaid?" exclaimed a gentleman, rushing half frantic down-stairs; "here's a man got into my room and swears he *will* dress in it."

"Oh! I begs pardon, sir," replied the chambermaid, trying to smooth him over, "we really are *so full*, sir, and I didn't think you'd be coming in so soon, sir."

"Waiter! Somebody has changed my place at dinner! I was next Mr. Walter Dale, and now they've put me below Mr. Barker—between him and Mr. Alcock: who the devil's done it?"

"Boots! Porter! Boots! run down to Mr. Ingledew's, the tailor's—you know him, don't you? Corner of Hill Street— just as you turn off the esplanade; and tell him he's sent me the wrong coat. Not half the size of my own—more like a strait-jacket than anything else. And here I desire Mrs. Kirton to send some ball gloves for me to try on—lemon colour or white— three and sixpenny ones."

"Lauk, I've come away and left Miss Eliza's stockings, I do declare!" exclaims Jemima Thirlwell, Miss Eliza Rippon's lady's maid, pale with fear, "what *shall* I do? Never was anything so unlucky—just took them to run my hand through and see they were all right, and left them hanging over the back of the chair. Know as well where they are as possible— but what's the use of that when they are ten miles off?"

"Waiter, what time's dinner?"

"Five o'clock, sir, and no waiting—Mr. Jorrocks swears he'll take the chair at five precisely, whether it's served or not," adds the waiter with a grin.

Then there was such work in the kitchen—Susan Straker, the cook, like all the sisterhood, was short in her temper, and severe and endless were the trials it underwent in consequence of the jingling and the tinkling of the bells calling away the chambermaids who were to have assisted her in the kitchen. Then Mr. Jorrocks deranged her whole system by insisting upon having a sucking-pig and roast goose that she intended for centre dishes, right under his nose at the top of the table; added to which, the fish was late in coming, and there was not half as much macaroni in the town as would make an inn dish.

"Now, Jun," said Mrs. Jorrocks to her loving spouse, taking a finishing look at our hero as he merged from his bed-room in the full dress uniform of his hunt, "see and conduct yourself like a gen'leman and with dignity, and, above all, keep *sober*. . . ."

And so we could continue with our anthology almost indefinitely if space permitted. The Inns have always exercised a special fascination over English writers, and it is not so far a cry from Johnson, Hazlitt, and Washington Irving to the redoubtable figures of Mr. Chesterton, Mr. Belloc, and Mr. Herbert, who in our own time stand ready, if the need arises, to take up cudgels in their defence against the attacks of prigs and puritans of every kind. The Inns are still fortunate in their protagonists, which, when one comes to think of it, is not surprising, since their mellow tradition is very much a part of the real England. Let us hope that for many years to come there will still be found writers to commemorate this tradition in the real English vintage prose and verse, of which the few excerpts we have quoted in this chapter provide such memorable and fascinating examples.

ENVOI

LINES WRITTEN AT AN INN

To thee, fair freedom, I retire,
From flattery, feasting, dice and din;
Nor art thou found in domes much higher
Than the lone cot or humble Inn.

'Tis here with boundless power I reign,
And every health which I begin,
Converts dull port to bright champagne;
For Freedom crowns it, at an Inn.

I fly from pomp, I fly from plate,
I fly from falsehood's specious grin;
Freedom I love, and form I hate,
And choose my lodgings at an Inn.

Here, waiter! take my sordid ore,
Which lacqueys else might hope to win;
It buys what Courts have not in store,
It buys me freedom, at an Inn.

And now once more I shape my way
Through rain or shine, through thick and thin,
Secure to meet, at close of day,
With kind reception at an Inn.

Whoe'er has travelled life's dull round,
Where'er his stages may have been,
May sigh to think how oft he found
The warmest welcome—at an Inn.

WILLIAM SHENSTONE.

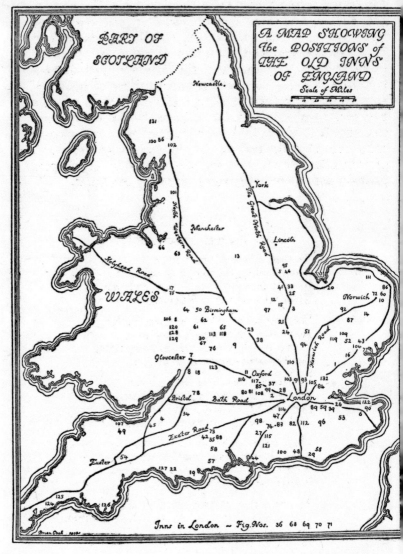

MAP SHOWING THE PRINCIPAL COACHING ROUTES, WITH THE
SITUATIONS OF THE INNS ILLUSTRATED (THE NUMERALS REFER
TO THE FIGURE NUMBERS OF THE ILLUSTRATIONS)

106 THE ANGEL, LUDLOW, SHROPSHIRE. Midland half-timber
and Georgian bays

107 THE LUTTRELL ARMS, DUNSTER, SOMERSET. The ivy-covered front of the ancient inn, with a glimpse of the Castle, village street, and Yarn-market

108 THE BRIDGE INN, SHILLINGFORD, BERKSHIRE. A delightful Thameside retreat
among old trees

109 THE ANGEL, LAVENHAM, SUFFOLK. A plastered
Georgian inn in the little East-Anglian weaving town

110 THE ROEBUCK, KNEBWORTH, HERTFORDSHIRE.
An unspoilt landmark on the Great North Road

111 THE BUCKINGHAMSHIRE ARMS, BLICKLING, NORFOLK.
Discreetly situated by the gates of the great house

112 THE CLAYTON ARMS, GODSTONE, SURREY. A great coaching
inn on the road to Lewes, formerly *The White Hart*

113   THE FERRY INN, FLADBURY, WORCESTERSHIRE.
A dignified Georgian landmark on Shakespeare's Avon

114 THE ANCHOR, WISLEY, SURREY. A charming riverside
alehouse on the Wey

115 THE WHITE HORSE, HASLEMERE, SURREY. A gentlemanly
frontage in neat Georgian brick

A SELECTED LIST OF NOTABLE INNS
FOR TOURING

The resources of England as a field for touring are as limitless as they are attractive. If the area to be covered seems at the first onset restricted to the visitor from overseas, and the whole countryside a reduced miniature to those accustomed to the vast spaces of the New World or the East, it is none the less an inexhaustible treasury for rambling. But a tour needs general if not detailed planning, which is fortunately far from difficult with the modern equivalent of the eighteenth-century road book. England is a country of countless miles of lanes and byroads, almost all nowadays of excellent or fair to passable surface, and the great delight of the discriminating tourist is to wander at will through their sinuous stretches from village green to secluded hamlet, along ridgeways, across gorsy commons, up above bracken-covered hillsides and over downs and wolds, touching the course of quiet brooks—unshackled by any cut-and-dried itinerary yet following a roughly worked course. It is entirely unnecessary in most parts of the country to hug for more than a few miles the canalised high road; for the small or moderate-sized car there is an infinity of village lanes, and even the big fellow can manage comfortably on the majority of by-roads. The motor or pedal cyclist can penetrate almost anywhere, and for him in such districts as the South-Western Counties or the Welsh Border is available a wealth of high-banked ferny farm lanes which lead to quiet hollows and unknown vantage-points of widespreading views. The hiker is free in addition of leagues of cart-tracks, green lanes, and footpaths leading into the very heart of the most sequestered landscapes, and he can easily widen his daily range of miles by a cunning use of the ramifying 'bus services or the jogging local branch line. All these will bring the traveller into the full enjoyment of unending stretches of unspoiled country,

with all its associations from the past, its fine sturdy old
buildings, and its mellow and gracious charm. Each
district has its own individuality and its own beauty,
whether in the rural Home Counties, the sweeping undulations of the Chilterns and Cotswolds, the long green
chalk ridges of the chalk from Wiltshire to the South-
Eastern seas, the quiet pastoral stretches of East Anglia,
the bolder outlines of the Midlands and South-West,
and the high fells, massive moors, and winding dales of
the North. There is no more amusing and remunerative
form of rambling than to wander in search of old inns;
it is not suggested that their wares should be sampled in
wholesale fashion, for an inn ramble is vastly different
from a 'pub crawl,' indeed its very opposite. Just as no one
really knows the lanes and by-roads of England, so nobody
dare claim to be acquainted with her innumerable inns, in
which are incorporated almost all the types of domestic
building of the past five centuries. The minor houses of
call exist in thousands; they front the wide stretches of
village greens; they stand as lonely shelters in deserted
uplands; they await you friendly on the outskirts of
country places, and they are hidden in the back lanes of
quiet backwater towns. Some, thatched and half-timbered,
are only distinguishable by their picture-sign and wooden
benches from the cottages that cluster round them (117–
119); others thrust out twin bay windows (26, 27)
through which the red-curtained lights shine welcoming
in the gathering dusk. Then there is the three-storey
Georgian brick inn at the entrance to the town, stolid
in bucolic dignity, with country carts and farm motors
pulled up outside. So we go on from the pleasant calm
of the Regency town inn (45) to the vast plastered
expanse of the grand hotel of the country town (47),
with the stately but faded Assembly Rooms attached.
Inside the country inn it is pleasantly shady and cool on
a hot day, and it is comfortable to draw round the log fire
on the brick hearth in the nipping weather of late autumn,
with a tall curving settle to ward off the draughts. There
are often shovel games and dart boards, with ancient
devices and relics of bygone years, and usually an atmo-

116 THE ROSE REVIVED, NEW BRIDGE, OXFORDSHIRE. Long a
private house, the little *Rose*, overlooking the infant Thames,
has lately blossomed anew as *The Rose Revived*

117 THE BARLEY MOW, LONG WITTENHAM, BERKSHIRE.
A small thatched alehouse in a Thameside village

118 THE BELL, ABBOTS SALFORD, WORCESTERSHIRE

119 THE FIVE BELLS, CAVENDISH, SUFFOLK (*recently demolished*).
Typical thatched alehouses of the West and East

120 THE BULL, LUDLOW, SHROPSHIRE.
Morning in the inn yard

sphere of ready friendliness; you are made free of the
village folk's racy chat, and can often glean items of
local life and scraps of history or tales of the past. At
no period have there been so many inns catering for the
visitors that the development of road travel has sent
scampering over the countryside. The road books of
the Automobile Association and similar societies provide
an excellent system of grading according to the number
of stars, to suit the tourist's pretensions and purse, just
as their map sheets are the lineal descendants of the

A CHIMNEY-CORNER AT 'THE WHITE HORSE,' EATON SOCON,
BEDFORDSHIRE

Ogilvy and Paterson coach books. The Trust Houses
and the hotels of the People's Refreshment House
Association, Surrey Trust, and similar bodies provide a
widespread range of comfortable hostelries with reliable
service. But a number of the village inns have themselves
taken up letting rooms to visitors, and can usually reach
a good standard of homely unpretentious comfort. Most
houses can rise to a plain tea, and many afford a tolerable
night's lodging at a pinch, but it must be realised that
many minor places will undertake nothing in the way of
catering or accommodation, and a request for anything

of the sort may be bluntly refused. A little discrimination is easily acquired, and in case of reluctance or doubtful reception it is best to withdraw promptly; don't expect much attention as a rule on the night of a club dinner, for instance, or the visit of a motoring rally; there is nearly always alternative accommodation. But be wary on bank-holiday week-ends, in the height of the August season, or at Christmas. There will occasionally be found grim and churlish landlords, who seem in their misanthropic attitude towards human nature to be the apostolic descendants of those embittered men in the coaching days who desired to revenge themselves on the race of mankind by "taking a pike" in their retirement. Mr. C. G. Harper, unrivalled in the extent of his wanderings and his writings, suggests that the irritating and inhospitable jingle of the 'Gate' sign:—

> This gate hangs well and hinders none
> Refresh and pay, then travel on,

is typical of this kind of temperament: "Hurry up with your drink, pay up and clear out; we don't want you hanging about here." It would be more tactful to word it: "Rest and Refresh!" A slightly less unfavourable version on a sign near Canterbury puts the doggerel into the mouth of the gratified customer:—

> I'm much refreshed; here, take your pay
> Be sure I'll call another day.

For touring generally nothing can better the Bartholo-mew's half-inch to the mile coloured maps, but for close work on by-lanes or footpaths these should be supple-mented by the one-inch coloured large sheet series of the Ordnance Survey. There are endless ways of working out interesting and original tours; it is a good idea to follow up the course of little known but beautiful rivers like the Teme or Lugg in the West Midlands, or the Colne, Windrush, or Evenlode in the Cotswolds; this involves a lot of up and down collar work—the lanes rarely keep the river valleys, but traverse the ridges, and

121 THE SPREAD EAGLE, MIDHURST, SUSSEX. The double frontage of this great inn provides an interesting contrast in periods

122   BELTINGE, KENT.   A fine old weather-boarded roadside inn.   Notice the typical Kentish oast-house behind

plunge up and down between the villages. Then a section of well-defined hill country can be thoroughly quartered by car or on foot, with emphatic scenic contrasts, as on the Quantocks or Mendips. Below the escarpments of the Berkshire Downs, Chilterns, or Cotswolds are clusters of interesting villages full of pleasant small inns (80, 81), and a ramble among these can be varied by a run to the top of the ridge or the little-populated upland country behind.

But if the inn explorer will have his disappointments he is bound to make exciting discoveries; many houses have ancient unspoiled backs, sometimes shut away behind façades of the dreariest nineteenth-century brick; such in East Anglia are often a jumble of half-timbered gables. *The Bull* at Ludlow has a fifteenth-century range of stabling (120), with its own stair giving on to St. Lawrence's churchyard. The Georgian *George* at West Wycombe has also a half-timber range at the back (p. 5). Many inn yards have escaped levelling into featureless modernisation, and remain straight out of coaching times, such as the range at Brentwood (132). The tendency to rebuild is steadily wiping out the old inns with all their associations. *The Flying Horse* at Kegworth and *The Five Bells* at Cavendish (119) have recently taken new shapes. The typical *Castle* at Wigmore has been burnt and a tin garage occupies the site. Hence it is well to visit the old places before they disappear. The surviving old style village inn is still sometimes a folk museum, otherwise lacking in the countryside. It may have ships in bottles, Toby jugs, clay pipes, an array of glittering brass, old sporting prints, and weird paintings from sold-up country houses. Not many country town inns keep their 'market ordinary,' no longer at a shilling, though the ancient sixpenny horse 'bus still plods clopping slowly from the remotely placed station, and occasionally 'Posting in all its Branches' is even yet proudly announced on its face. A visit to the kitchen of such a place is a joy, with its spit racks, huge hams hanging on hooks, a great open range, and perhaps an ancient staircase. But beware of being caught by a

P

STAIRCASE IN THE YARD OF THE FORMER
'PLUME OF FEATHERS,' SALISBURY

virago landlady or termagant manageress, a type occasionally surviving with aggressive Victorian instincts of
propriety.

123 THE MILL INN, WITHINGTON, GLOUCESTERSHIRE. A delightful waterside group in the South Cotswolds

128 PEMBRIDGE, HEREFORDSHIRE. The half-timber
New Inn by the market-place

129 THE RED LION, WEOBLEY, HEREFORDSHIRE. In the
heart of the half-timber country

In rambling one comes across such a piece as the *Plume of Feathers* yard at Salisbury, with its twisting stairway preserved though industrialised, and its name transferred to a nondescript tavern by the station. It is a joy to come on such a galleried Regency yard as *The Eagle* at Cambridge. Sometimes old work comes to light, as in the remarkable Tudor mural paintings at *The White Swan*, Stratford-on-Avon (105 A & B) now illustrating the story of Tobit from the Apocrypha. *The Rose and Crown*, Ashdon, near Saffron Walden, has

THE TAP-ROOM FIREPLACE AT
'THE WHITE HART,' BLETCHINGLEY, SURREY

a complete painted room of the seventeenth century hidden away. Occasionally casual exploration is rendered worth while by the discovery of a gem, typical in itself and lovely in its setting. *The George* at Hurstbourne Tarrant cross-roads is a charming small Georgian house, with square many-paned bay window, appropriate yard and backs, and a gaily painted sign. It witnessed the start of Cobbett for many of his 'Rural Rides' from its red brick opposite neighbour.

The smaller inns have often a local flavour when not turned into smart roadhouses like *The Windmill*

Ewhurst, Surrey, or *The Bear* at Rodborough, near Stroud, where it is interesting to trace the amazing transformation of the tiny roadside Cotswold house of Ralph Nevill's drawing to the great caravanserai of to-day. The village public-houses of a district have often a distinct character of their own—the Wealden village inns run to chimney corners and wide-open hearths, with the local fireback and dogs, and often a good working potcrane. In the Chilterns the landlord often works at the district craft of chair-turning, as at *The Fox* at Christmas Common and *The Pheasant* beyond Bledlow Ridge, where he will produce you a perfectly shaped chair-leg in five minutes. But many country town inns abound remarkably in endlessly rambling corridors, with many flights of stairs and a plan of tangled complexity, of which Dickens gleefully took advantage in the incidents at the Ipswich *White Horse* in *Pickwick*. At an angle are sometimes found hot-water cans in massed formation, or long lines of numbered jangling bedroom bells. Such ramifications may be found at *The Crown*, Worcester, and *The Maid's Head*, Norwich, where the passages seem designed for a game at hide and seek for a whole party. Then there are the isolated inns of the Northern moors, whose bleak exteriors reveal nothing of the homely comfort usually to be enjoyed within. Again, there are the houses plumped down in the saddle of a pass, or on the highest point of a long ascent, like *The Puesdown*, at 800 feet in the Cotswolds on the Oxford–Cheltenham road, or the little *Fish* on the very edge of the escarpment on Broadway Hill (p. 43). The inns of the land are infinite in variety, and their study and exploration is a never-ending pursuit. As they are the centres of the people's social life, from the small hamlet to the great cities, they can reveal the atmosphere of countryside and town, and throw much light on the feelings, character, and spirit of the English people, their steady patience, their calm steadfastness, and their quiet but lively sense of humour and enjoyment.

130 THE SWAN, GRASMERE, WESTMORLAND

131 THE PHEASANT, BASSENTHWAITE, CUMBERLAND.
Two snug Lakeland inns in their mountain settings

132   THE WHITE HART, BRENTWOOD, ESSEX.   The weather-boarded stabling of the inn yard

A SELECTED LIST OF NOTABLE INNS

This list makes no claim to be complete or even exhaustive; it can only give a representative selection, for the number of interesting old houses is enormous and beyond reckoning. This is a list of inns of interest, not necessarily for visiting purposes.

BEDFORDSHIRE
Ampthill: *White Hart*
Barford (Gt.): *Swan*
Bedford: *Red Lion—Swan*
Biggleswade: *Swan*
Dunstable: *Sugar Loaf*
Eaton Socon: *White Horse*
Elstow: *Swan*
Leighton Buzzard: *Swan*
Tempsford: *Anchor*
Turvey: *Five Fishes*
Woburn: *Bedford Arms*

BERKSHIRE
Abingdon: *Lion—King's Head & Bell*
East Hagbourne: *Fleur de Lis*
Faringdon: *Bell—Crown*
Hartford Bridge: *White Lion*
Hungerford: *Black Bear—Three Swans*
Hurley: *Bell*
Lambourn: *Red Lion*
Long Wittenham: *Barley Mow*
Maidenhead: *Bear*
Newbury: *Chequers—Jack o' Newbury—Pelican*
Pangbourne: *George—Swan*
Reading: *Ship*
Shillingford: *Bridge*
Stanton: *Fox & Hounds*
Thatcham: *King's Head—White Hart*
Theale: *Old Angel*
Wallingford: *George—Lamb*
Waltham St. Lawrence: *Bell*
Wantage: *Bear*
Windsor: *Star & Garter—White Hart*

BUCKINGHAMSHIRE
Amersham: *Crown—Griffin*
Aylesbury: *Bell—George—King's Head*
Beaconsfield: *Royal Saracen—Royal White Hart*

BUCKINGHAMSHIRE—*continued*
Bierton: *Red Lion*
Buckingham: *Swan & Castle—White Hart*
Chalfont St. Peter: *Greyhound*
Chesham: *Crown—George*
Colnbrook: *Ostrich*
Denham: *Swan*
High Wycombe: *Falcon—Red Lion*
Marlow: *Chequers—Compleat Angler—Crown*
Newport Pagnell: *Anchor—Swan*
Olney: *Bull*
Princes Risborough: *George & Dragon*
Stony Stratford: *Bull—Cock*
Stratford, Fenny: *Bull—Cock—Swan*
Wendover: *Nag's Head—Packhorse—Red Lion*
West Wycombe: *George*
Whitchurch: *White Hart*

CAMBRIDGESHIRE
Cambridge: *Blue Boar—Bull—Castle—Eagle—Red Lion—Three Tuns*
Chatteris: *Old George*
Ely: *Bell—Lamb*
Grantchester: *Red Lion*
March: *Old Griffin*
Royston: *Bull*
Wisbech: *Rose & Crown—Ship*

CHESHIRE
Alderley Edge: *De Trafford Arms*
Altrincham: *Unicorn*
Brereton: *Boar's Head*
Cheadle: *George & Dragon—White Hart*
Chester: *Bear & Billet—Falcon—Feathers*
Congleton: *Bull's Head—Lion & Swan*
Knutsford: *Angel—Royal George*
Macclesfield: *Macclesfield Arms*

Q

CHESHIRE—*continued*
  Nantwich: *Crown—Lamb*
  Plumbley: *Smoker*
  Sandbach: *Bear—Old Hall*
  School's Hill: *Old Bull*
  Tabley: *Windmill*
  Tarporley: *Alvanley Arms—Swan*

CORNWALL
  Bodinnick: *Old Ferry*
  Bodmin Moor: *Bol Ventor*
  Boscastle: *Wellington*
  Bude: *Falcon*
  Callington: *Golding's Hotel*
  Falmouth: *Royal*
  Fowey: *Lugger*
  Helston: *Angel*
  Lands End: *First & Last House*
  Launceston: *Castle—King's Arms—
    White Hart*
  Liskeard: *Stag—Webb's*
  Lostwithiel: *Royal Talbot*
  Mousehole: *Keigwin Arms*
  Penzance: *Star*
  St. Austell: *Queen's Head*
  St. Ives: *Golden Lion—Tregenna
    Castle*
  Stoke Climsland: *Half Moon*
  Truro: *King's Arms—Red Lion—
    Royal*

CUMBERLAND
  Bassenthwaite: *Pheasant*
  Brampton: *White Lion*
  Carlisle: *Crown & Mitre—Red Lion*
  Cockermouth: *Glebe*
  Egremont: *King's Arms*
  Keswick: *Old George—Pheasant*
  Penrith: *Crown*
  Wigton: *Kildare*

DERBYSHIRE
  Ashbourne: *Green Man*
  Bakewell: *Rutland Arms*
  Buxton: *George—Old Hall—Shake-
    speare*
  Chapel-en-le-Frith: *King's Arms*
  Derby: *Midland*
  Dovedale: *Black Man's Head—
    Green Man*
  Glossop: *Norfolk Arms*
  Ilkeston: *Rutland*
  Matlock: *Crown*
  Rowsley: *Peacock*

DEVONSHIRE
  Ashburton: *Golden Lion*
  Axminster: *George*
  Barnstaple: *Old Ship—Royal*
  Bickleigh: *New Inn*
  Bicton: *King's Arms*
  Bideford: *Royal—Old Ship*
  Bovey Tracey: *Dolphin*
  Chagford: *Three Crowns*
  Chudleigh: *Clifford Arms*
  Clovelly: *New Inn*
  Crediton: *Ship*
  Dartmoor: *Warren House Inn*
  Dartmouth: *Raleigh—Royal Castle*
  Devonport: *Royal Hotel*
  Dulverton: *Lamb—Red Lion*
  Exeter: *Clarendon—London—Royal
    Clarence*
  Exmouth: *London—Royal Beacon—
    Thorn*
  Holsworthy: *White Hart*
  Honiton: *Dolphin (Banfield's)*
  Ivybridge: *London*
  Kingsbridge: *King's Arms*
  Moreton Hampstead: *White Hart*
  Newton Abbot: *Globe*
  Okehampton: *White Hart*
  Plymouth: *Royal*
  Princetown: *Duchy — Plume of
    Feathers*
  Slapton: *Sands*
  South Molton: *George—Unicorn*
  Star Cross: *Courtenay Arms*
  Tavistock: *Bedford*
  Teignmouth: *Royal*
  Tiverton: *Angel*
  Topsham: *Salutation*
  Totnes: *Royal Seven Stars—Somerset
    Arms*

DORSET
  Beaminster: *White Hart*
  Blandford: *Crown*
  Bridport: *Bridport Arms—Bull—
    Greyhound*
  Corfe: *Greyhound*
  Dorchester: *Antelope—King's Arms
    —White Hart*
  Lyme Regis: *Royal Lion—Three Cups*
  Poole: *Antelope—King Charles—
    London*
  Shaftesbury: *Grosvenor*
  Sherborne: *Digby*

DORSET—*continued*
  Swanage: *Ship*
  Wareham: *Black Bear*
  Wimborne: *Coach & Horses—Crown
    —King's Head*

DURHAM
  Barnard Castle: *King's Head*
  Darlington: *King's Head*
  Durham: *Rose & Crown—Three
    Tuns*
  Middleton-in-Teesdale: *Cleveland
    Arms*

ESSEX
  Ashdon: *Rose & Crown*
  Braintree: *Horns—White Hart*
  Brentwood: *Fleece—White Hart*
  Chelmsford: *Lion & Lamb—White
    Hart*
  Chigwell: *King's Head (Maypole)*
  Colchester: *Cups—George—Marquis
    of Granby — Red Lion — Three
    Horseshoes*
  Dunmow: *Saracen's Head*
  Harwich: *White Hart*
  Maldon: *Blue Boar—King's Head*
  Ongar: *King's Head*
  Paglesham: *Plough & Sail*
  Saffron Walden: *Rose & Crown*
  Southend: *Royal Hotel*
  Thaxted: *Swan*
  Waltham: *White Hart*
  Waltham Cross: *Four Swans*
  Witham: *Spread Eagle—White Hart*

GLOUCESTERSHIRE
  Bibury: *Swan*
  Bourton-on-the-Water: *New Inn*
  Bristol: *Royal Western Hotel*
  Cheltenham: *Fleece — Plough —
    Queen's—Royal*
  Chipping Campden: *Lygon Arms—
    Noel Arms*
  Chipping Sodbury: *Cross Hands*
  Dursley: *Bell—Castle*
  Gloucester: *Fleece — Greyhound —
    New Inn*
  Lechlade: *New Inn*
  Moreton in Marsh: *Redesdale Arms
    —Royal*
  Northleach: *Wheatsheaf*
  Stow on the Wold: *Talbot—Unicorn*

GLOUCESTERSHIRE—*continued*
  Tewkesbury: *Bear—Bell—Berkeley
    Arms—Hop Pole—Sun—Swan—
    Wheatsheaf*
  Thornbury: *Swan*
  Winchcomb: *George—Old Corner
    Cupboard*
  Withington: *Mill Inn*

HAMPSHIRE
  Alresford: *Swan*
  Alton: *Swan*
  Andover: *Star & Garter—White
    Hart*
  Basingstoke: *Red Lion*
  Bishop's Waltham: *Crown*
  Cadnam: *Inn*
  Christchurch: *King's Arms*
  Fareham: *Red Lion*
  Hartley Row: *Lamb*
  Hinton Admiral: *Cat & Fiddle*
  Hook: *White Hart*
  Hurstbourne Tarrant: *George*
  Liphook: *Angel—Royal Anchor*
  Lymington: *Angel—Old Toll House*
  Lyndhurst: *Crown—Stag*
  Odiham: *George—Tuns*
  Petersfield: *Red Lion*
  Portsmouth: *George*
  Ringwood: *Crown—White Hart*
  Romsey: *Dolphin—White Horse*
  Shanklin: *Crab & Lobster*
  Southampton: *Dolphin*
  Twyford: *King's Arms*
  Whitchurch: *White Hart*
  Winchester: *George—Hostel of God
    Begot*

HEREFORDSHIRE
  Bromyard: *Falcon—Hop Pole*
  Hereford: *Green Dragon—Mitre*
  Ledbury: *Feathers—Horse Shoe—
    Royal Oak*
  Leominster: *Royal Oak—Talbot*
  Pembridge: *New Inn, by Market Hall*
  Ross: *King's Head—Man of Ross—
    Royal—Swan*
  Weobley: *Old Unicorn—Red Lion*

HERTFORDSHIRE
  Baldock: *Rose & Crown*
  Barley: *Fox & Hounds*
  Barnet: *Hart's Horns—Red Lion*

HERTFORDSHIRE—*continued*
Berkhampstead: *King's Arms—Swan*
Bishops Stortford: *Chequers—George—White Horse*
Buntingford: *George & Dragon*
Digswell Hill: *Waggon & Horses*
Hatfield: *Eight Bells—Red Lion—Salisbury Arms*
Hertford: *Blue Boy—Dimsdale Arms—Green Dragon*
Hitchin: *Cock—Coopers' Arms—Sun—Three Tuns*
Hoddesdon: *Bull*
Knebworth: *Roebuck*
Redbourn: *Bull*
Royston: *Bull—Crown*
St. Albans: *Fighting Cocks—George—Peahen—Red Lion—White Hart*
St. Michaels, St. Albans: *Black Lion*
Tring: *Bell—Rose & Crown*
Ware: *Saracen's Head*
Water End: *Red Lion*
Watford: *Clarendon—Essex Arms—George—Rose & Crown*

HUNTINGDONSHIRE
Buckden: *Falcon—George—Lion*
Huntingdon: *Bridge—George—Woolpack*
St. Neots: *Cross Keys*
Sawtry: *Globe*
Stilton: *Bell*

KENT
Boughton Aluph: *Flying Horse*
Bromley: *Royal Bell*
Canterbury: *Falstaff—Flying Horse—Fountain—Queen Elizabeth—Rose—Sun*
Cobham: *Leather Bottle*
Cranbrook: *George—Chequers*
Dartford: *Bull*
Dover: *Ship*
Farnborough: *Tumble Down Dick*
Faversham: *Ship*
Gad's Hill: *Falstaff*
Great Mongeham: *Three Horseshoes*
Otford: *Bull*
Poundsbridge: *Inn*
Rochester: *Bull—George*
Sandwich: *Bell*
Sarre: *Crown*

KENT—*continued*
Sevenoaks: *Royal Crown—Royal Oak—White Hart*
Shoreham: *George*
Sittingbourne: *Bull—Red Lion*
Speldhurst: *George & Dragon*
Tenterden: *White Lion*
Tonbridge: *Angel—Chequers—Rose & Crown*
Tunbridge Wells: *Castle*
Westbere: *Yew Tree*
Westerham: *George & Dragon—King's Arms*
Wingham: *Lion*

LANCASHIRE
Accrington: *Hargreave Arms*
Blackburn: *Old Bull—White Bull*
Burnley: *Bull—Old Sparrow Hawk—Thorn*
Clitheroe: *Swan & Royal*
Coniston: *Sun—Waterhead*
Garstang: *Royal Oak*
Lancaster: *County—King's Arms*
Lytham: *Clifton Arms*
Preston: *Bull & Royal*
Ribchester: *White Bull*
Sale: *Brooklands*
Todmorden: *White Hart*
Ulverston: *Sun*

LEICESTERSHIRE
Ashby-de-la-Zouch: *Royal*
Hinckley: *George*
Leicester: *Bell—George—Stag & Pheasant—Wyvern*
Loughborough: *King's Head—Old Bull's Head*
Lutterworth: *Denbigh Arms—Hind*
Market Harborough: *Angel—Peacock—Three Swans*
Melton Mowbray: *George*

LINCOLNSHIRE
Barton: *George*
Boston: *Red Lion—White Hart*
Bourn: *Angel—Bull*
Brigg: *Angel*
Caistor: *Red Lion*
Crowland: *George*
Gainsborough: *White Hart*
Grantham: *Angel—Beehive—George*
Great Grimsby: *Ship*

LINCOLNSHIRE—*continued*
  Holbeach: *Chequers*
  Horncastle: *Bull—Red Lion*
  Lincoln: *Saracen's Head—Spread Eagle—White Hart*
  Louth: *King's Head*
  Market Deeping: *New Inn*
  Scunthorpe: *Blue Bell*
  Skegness: *Lion*
  Sleaford: *Bristol Arms—White Hart*
  Spalding: *Red Lion—White Hart*
  Spilsbury: *George—White Hart*
  Stamford: *George—Stamford Hotel*

LONDON
  Aldgate: *Hoop & Grapes*
  Chiswick: *Lamb & Flag*
  Fleet Street: *Cheshire Cheese*
  Greenwich: *Ship*
  Hammersmith: *Black Lion—Doves*
  Hampstead: *Bull & Bush—Flask—Jack Straw's Castle—Spaniards*
  Limehouse: *Grapes*
  Mayfair: *Running Footman*
  Southwark: *George*
  Wapping: *Prospect of Whitby*

MIDDLESEX
  Edgware: *Chandos Arms*
  Gannick Corner: *Duke of York*
  Highgate: *Flask*
  Isleworth: *London Apprentice*
  Southall: *Whitehall*
  Uxbridge: *Crown & Treaty*

NORFOLK
  Attleborough: *Angel—Griffin*
  Blickling: *Buckinghamshire Arms*
  Cromer: *Old Red Lion*
  Diss: *Crown*
  Downham Market: *Castle—Crown*
  East Dereham: *King's Arms*
  Fakenham: *Crown—Lion*
  Great Yarmouth: *Angel*
  Harleston: *Swan*
  Heigham: *Dolphin*
  Holt: *Feathers*
  Horning: *Ferry*
  Hunstanton: *Globe—Golden Lion*
  King's Lynn: *Duke's Head—Globe*
  Norwich: *Bell—Briton's Arms—Castle—Maid's Head—Sir Garnet Wolsey*
  Scole: *White Hart*

NORFOLK—*continued*
  Swaffham: *George*
  Thetford: *Anchor—Bell*
  Wells: *Crown*
  Wymondham: *Green Dragon—King's Head*

NORTHAMPTONSHIRE
  Aynho: *Cartwright Arms*
  Brackley: *Crown*
  Daventry: *Saracen's Head—Wheatsheaf*
  Deene: *Sea Horse*
  Gretton: *White Hart*
  Kettering: *George—Royal*
  Northampton: *Angel—Cock—Peacock—Plough—Ram*
  Oundle: *Talbot—White Lion*
  Peterborough: *Angel*
  Rockingham: *Sondes Arms*
  Towcester: *Folly—Pomfret Arms—Talbot*
  Wansford: *Haycock*
  Weldon Magna: *King's Arms*
  Wellingborough: *Angel—Hind*

NORTHUMBERLAND
  Alnwick: *Plough—Star—White Swan*
  Belford: *Blue Bell*
  Berwick-on-Tweed: *King's Arms*
  Blanchland: *Crewe Arms*
  Hexham: *Abbey—Royal*

NOTTINGHAMSHIRE
  East Retford: *White Hart*
  Newark: *Clinton Arms—Ram—White Horse*
  Nottingham: *Black Boy—Flying Horse—George*
  Ollerton: *Hop Pole*
  Southwell: *Saracen's Head*
  Tuxford: *Newcastle Arms*
  Worksop: *Lion—Royal*

OXFORDSHIRE
  Banbury: *Red Lion—Reindeer—White Lion*
  Burford: *Bull*
  Bicester: *Crown*
  Benson: *Castle—Crown*
  Chipping Norton: *Crown & Anchor—White Hart*
  Clifton Hampden: *Barley Mow*

OXFORDSHIRE—*continued*
  Deddington: *Unicorn*
  Dorchester: *George—Golden Cross—White Hart*
  Ewelme: *Lamb*
  Godstow: *Trout*
  Goring and Streatley: *Miller of Mansfield—Swan*
  Henley: *Angel — Bull — Catherine Wheel—Little White Hart—Red Lion*
  New Bridge: *Rose Revived*
  Tetsworth: *Swan*
  Thame: *Hog's Head—Spread Eagle*
  Witney: *Marlborough Arms*
  Woodstock: *Bear*

RUTLANDSHIRE
  Oakham: *Crown—George*
  Uppingham: *Crown—Falcon*

SHROPSHIRE
  Bridgnorth: *Crown—Falcon—King's Arms—Swan*
  Church Stretton: *Longsword*
  Ellesmere: *Black Lion*
  Ludlow: *Angel—Bull—Feathers*
  Market Drayton: *Corbet Arms*
  Much Wenlock: *Gaskell Arms*
  Newport: *Barley Mow*
  Oswestry: *Wynnstay*
  Shrewsbury: *Crown—Dun Cow—King's Head—Lion—Plough—Post Office—Raven—Unicorn*
  Wellington: *Charlton Arms—Wrekin*
  Wem: *Castle—White Horse*
  Whitchurch: *Swan*

SOMERSET
  Axbridge: *George*
  Bath: *Angel—York House*
  Bridgwater: *Royal Clarence—White Hart*
  Chard: *George*
  Crewkerne: *George*
  Dunster: *Luttrell Arms*
  Frome: *Crown—George*
  Glastonbury: *Crown—George (Pilgrims' Inn)*
  Ilminster: *George*
  Minehead: *Plume of Feathers—Wellington*

SOMERSET—*continued*
  Norton St. Philip: *George*
  Porlock: *Ship*
  Shepton Mallet: *Hare & Hounds*
  Taunton: *Castle*
  Wells: *Mitre—Red Lion—Star—Swan*
  Wincanton: *Bear—Greyhound*
  Winsford: *Royal Oak*
  Yeovil: *Mermaid—Pen Mill—Three Choughs*

STAFFORDSHIRE
  Burton-upon-Trent: *White Hart*
  Eccleshall: *Crown—King's Arms*
  Himley: *Crooked House*
  Leek: *George—Red Lion*
  Lichfield: *Four Crosses—George—King's Head—Swan*
  Longton: *Crown & Anchor*
  Newcastle-under-Lyme: *Borough Arms*
  Penkridge: *Littleton Arms—White Hart*
  Rugeley: *Shrewsbury Arms*
  Stafford: *Swan—Vine*
  Tamworth: *Castle—Peel Arms*
  Uttoxeter: *White Hart*

SUFFOLK
  Aldburgh: *Railway*
  Bungay: *King's Head*
  Bury St. Edmunds: *Angel—Half Moon*
  Cavendish: *George*
  Chelmondiston: *Butt & Oyster*, Pin Mill
  Eye: *White Lion*
  Framlingham: *Crown*
  Ipswich: *Crown & Anchor—Great White Horse—Half Moon—Neptune*
  Kersey: *Bell—White Horse*
  Lavenham: *Angel—Swan*
  Long Melford: *Bull—Castle*
  Lowestoft: *Crown—Royal*
  Martlesham: *Lion*
  Newmarket: *Crown—Rutland Arms—White Hart*
  Saxmundham: *Bell—White Hart*
  Stanton: *Rose & Crown*
  Stowmarket: *Fox—King's Head*
  Sudbury: *Rose & Crown*

SUFFOLK—*continued*
Wickham Market: *White Hart*
Woodbridge: *Bell—Crown*

SURREY
Bletchingley: *Stag—White Hart*
Charlwood: *Half Moon*
Chertsey: *Crown*
Chiddingfold: *Crown*
Cobham: *White Lion*
Croydon: *Greyhound*
Dorking: *Red Lion—Star & Garter
—White Horse*
Epsom: *King's Head*
Esher: *Bear*
Farnham: *Bush—Jolly Farmer—Lion
& Lamb*
Godalming: *Angel—King's Arms*
Godstone: *Clayton Arms*
Guildford: *Angel—Lion*
Haslemere: *White Horse*
Kingston: *Sun*
Kingston Vale: *Plough*
Leatherhead: *Swan*
Ockley: *Red Lion*
Oxted: *Bell*
Reigate: *Swan—White Hart*
Ripley: *Anchor—Talbot*
Shere: *White Horse*
Sutton: *Cock*
Wisley: *Anchor*
Witley: *White Hart*

SUSSEX
Alfriston: *Market Cross—Star*
Battle: *George—Pilgrims' Hostel*
Brighton: *Bedford—Old Ship*
Chichester: *Anchor & Dolphin*
Crawley: *George*
Cuckfield: *King's Head*
East Grinstead: *Dorset Arms*
Felpham: *Fox*
Fittleworth: *Swan*
Hailsham: *George*
Horsham: *Anchor—Black Horse—
King's Head*
Lewes: *Crown—White Hart*
Mayfield: *Middle House*
Midhurst: *Angel—Spread Eagle*
Newhaven: *Bridge*
Petworth: *Swan*
Robertsbridge: *Seven Stars*
Rye: *Mermaid*

SUSSEX—*continued*
Sedlescombe: *Queen's Head*
Steyning: *Chequers*
Uckfield: *Maiden's Head*

WARWICKSHIRE
Alcester: *Globe*
Atherstone: *Red Lion*
Bidford: *Falcon*
Coventry: *King's Head*
Kenilworth: *King's Arms & Castle
—Queen & Castle*
Leamington: *Crown*
Leamington Spa: *Regent*
Nuneaton: *Gull*
Rugby: *Royal George—Three Horse-
shoes*
Southam: *Craven Arms*
Stratford-on-Avon: *Falcon—Garrick
— Red Horse — Golden Lion —
Shakespeare—Swan's Nest—White
Swan*
Warwick: *Crown—Warwick Arms
—Woolpack*

WESTMORLAND
Appleby: *King's Head—Tufton Arms*
Askham: *Queen's Head*
Brough: *Castle—George*
Grasmere: *Red Lion—Swan*
Kendal: *King's Arms*
Kirby Lonsdale: *Royal*
Kirkby Stephen: *Black Bull—King's
Arms*
Kirkstone Pass: *Traveller's Rest*

WILTSHIRE
Alderbury: *Green Dragon*
Amesbury: *George*
Bradford-on-Avon: *Swan*
Castle Combe: *Castle*
Chippenham: *Angel*
Corsham: *Methuen Arms*
Cricklade: *White Hart*
Devizes: *Bear*
Malmesbury: *Bell*
Marlborough: *Castle & Ball—Five
Alls*
Melksham: *King's Arms*
Mere: *Ship*
Pewsey: *Greyhound*
Salisbury: *Crown—George—Haunch
of Venison—Red Lion—White Hart*

WILTSHIRE—*continued*
Swindon: *Goddard Arms*—*King's Arms*
Trowbridge: *George*
Warminster: *Bath Arms*
Wilton: *Pembroke Arms*

WORCESTERSHIRE
Abbot's Salford: *Bell*
Bewdley: *George*
Broadway: *Fish*—*Lygon Arms*
Bromsgrove: *Golden Cross*
Chaddesley Corbett: *Talbot*
Cleeve Prior: *King's Head*
Droitwich: *Swan*
Evesham: *Crown*
Fladbury: *Ferry*
Great Malvern: *Beauchamp*
Inkberrow: *Old Bull*
Kidderminster: *Lion*
King's Norton: *Queen's Head*
Ombersley: *Half-Way House*—*King's Arms*
Pershore: *Royal Three Tuns*
Redditch: *Unicorn*
Stourport: *Swan*
Tenbury: *Swan*
Upton-on-Severn: *White Hart*—*White Lion*
Worcester: *Crown*—*Pheasant*—*Star*

YORKSHIRE
Barnby Moor: *Bel.*
Bawtry: *Crown*
Bedale: *Black Swan*

YORKSHIRE—*continued*
Beverley: *Beverley Arms*
Boroughbridge: *Three Greyhounds*
Doncaster: *Reindeer*
Great Driffield: *Bell*—*Buck*
Guisborough: *Ward Arms*
Harrogate: *George*
Ilkley: *Crescent*
Leeds: *Boar's Head*—*Golden Lion*—*Griffin*
Leyburn: *Golden Lion*
Market Weighton: *Londesborough*
Northallerton: *Golden Lion*
Otley: *Black Horse*—*Royal White Horse*
Pickering: *Black Swan* — *White Swan*
Pocklington: *Feathers*
Pontefract: *Red Lion*
Richmond: *King's Head*
Ripon: *Unicorn*
Rotherham: *Crown*
Sedbergh: *Bull*—*White Hart*
Selby: *George*
Settle: *Golden Lion*
Skipton: *Black Horse*—*Ship*
Tadcaster: *Londesborough*
Thirsk: *Fleece*—*Three Tuns*
Wakefield: *Strafford Arms*—*White Horse*
Whitby: *Angel*
Witherby: *Angel*—*Brunswick*
Yarm-on-Tees: *George & Dragon*
York: *Black Swan*—*Harker's*—*Windmill*—*White Swan*

INDEX

(The numerals in italics denote the *figure numbers* of photographic illustrations.
Text drawings are referred to under their page numbers)

A Selected List of
BATSFORD BOOKS
relating to

Architecture, Fine and Decorative Art, Interior Decoration, Gardens, Social History, Crafts, Applied Science, Engineering, etc.

Published by B. T. BATSFORD LTD.

Booksellers and Publishers by appointment to H.M. The Queen

15 North Audley Street, London

CONTENTS

NOTE.—This list comprises about 190 books on the subjects shown above from Batsford's main catalogue, in which are listed some 600 odd titles. It is intended to form a representative selection for the use of readers, but those interested in any particular subject should obtain the main catalogue (which will be sent post free on request), which comprises a much wider range of titles under every head. Fully illustrated prospectuses of most books can also be sent on request. Patrons are reminded that Batsford's new premises are at 15 North Audley Street, London, W.1, one minute from Oxford Street, on the main thoroughfare leading to Grosvenor Square, two minutes' walk from either Bond Street or Marble Arch Stations on the Central London Railway, where their immense stock of books, old and new, English and foreign, with prints, pictures, etc., can be inspected at leisure in the large and beautifully-fitted new showrooms. *Telephone Mayfair* 6118 ; *Accounts and Production, Mayfair* 4337. *Cables: Batsfordia, London. Telegrams: Batsford, Audley, London.*

A full index of the books contained in this list arranged alphabetically under the names of authors, is given on page 32.

List F. 50m. 3/34.

THE CATHEDRALS OF ENGLAND

By HARRY BATSFORD and CHARLES FRY. The letterpress consists of a rapid but comprehensive Introduction, followed by a short, clear description of each cathedral, its situation, history, architecture and romance. There are 133 illustrations from new photographs, which form a superb series, far in advance of anything yet produced on the subject. There are also a colour Frontispiece from an old drawing by F. Mackenzie, and some 30 Line Sketches in the text by BRIAN COOK. The book is the ideal guide for the modern tourist, untechnical but absolutely reliable, superbly produced and illustrated. Demy 8vo, cloth, lettered. 7s. 6d. net.

THE ENGLISH VILLAGE

By SIR JOHN SQUIRE. This book is the work not only of a famous man of letters, but of one who has fought unceasingly for the preservation of the English countryside, of which his knowledge is extraordinarily wide and comprehensive. As a treatise on the English Village, its life, character, history and architecture, it will be appreciated by all who love the tranquil charm and fine old craftsmanship of these beautiful survivals. There are 130 superb illustrations from new Photographs and twenty Drawings in the text by SYDNEY R. JONES. Demy 8vo, cloth, lettered. 7s. 6d. net.

THE OLD INNS OF ENGLAND

By A. E. RICHARDSON, F.S.A. This volume constitutes a comprehensive survey of the fine old inns that are one of the most attractive features of the English towns and villages. It is a fascinating subject, embracing the whole life of the roads through England's history, and Professor Richardson has done full justice to it in a letterpress that is full of knowledge and robust humour. It is illustrated by 130 fine new Photographs of inns, medieval and later, in stone or timber, and there are in addition 20 Line Drawings by BRIAN COOK. The book is an indispensable possession to the motorist. Demy 8vo, cloth, lettered. 7s. 6d. net.

THE FACE OF SCOTLAND

A Pictorial Review of its Scenery: Hills, Glens, Lochs, Coast, Islands, Moors, etc., with Old Buildings, Castles, Churches, etc. Including a brief review of Topography, History and Characteristics. By HARRY BATSFORD and CHARLES FRY, with a foreword by JOHN BUCHAN, C.H., M.P. With 130 splendid illustrations, from specially selected Photographs, many hitherto unpublished, a Frontispiece in colour from a Water-colour by W. RUSSELL FLINT, R.A., and numerous Line Drawings in the text by BRIAN COOK. Demy 8vo, cloth, lettered. 7s. 6d. net.

THE "ENGLISH LIFE" SERIES

THE LANDSCAPE OF ENGLAND

By CHARLES BRADLEY FORD. With a Foreword by Professor G. M. TREVELYAN, O.M., M.A., F.S.A., etc. An attractive, popular, yet systematic and informative survey under 5 main divisions: North, Midlands, East, South-East, and West Country. With 135 fine Photographic Illustrations, mostly full-page and largely unpublished, including also a coloured Frontispiece, 25 Pen Drawings and 6 Maps, by BRIAN COOK. Large 8vo, cloth, lettered. 12s. 6d. net.

"The varied beauties of English landscape are reflected with unusual charm in this treasurable volume. It would seem impossible, indeed, to overpraise the quality of the artistry and skill which has gone to the making of this book. The volume as a whole has been well planned ; it is a truly remarkable and appealing production."—*Liverpool Daily Post.*

THE "ENGLISH LIFE" SERIES—(continued)

HOMES AND GARDENS OF ENGLAND

By HARRY BATSFORD, Hon. A.R.I.B.A., and CHARLES FRY. With a Foreword by LORD CONWAY of Allington. An attractive, popular, yet informative survey from the Middle Ages to Victorian Times of old Country
Houses and their Gardens. Containing 175 Photographic Illustrations, a
Frontispiece in colour by SYDNEY R. JONES, and numerous Line Drawings
and Engravings in the text. Large 8vo, cloth, lettered. 12s. 6d. net.

"It is difficult to avoid the appearance of adulation in giving any account of this
superbly illustrated production, which at 12s. 6d. gives every indication of philanthropy.
The accompanying text is a model of grace and brevity, and the work provides not only
an excellent grounding, but its possession is certain to be a continued delight."—*The
Bookfinder Illustrated.*

THE ENGLISH COUNTRYSIDE

By ERNEST C. PULBROOK. A Review of some of its Aspects, Features,
and Attractions. With 126 Illustrations from Photographs, and a Pencil
Frontispiece by A. E. NEWCOMBE. New and cheaper impression. Large 8vo,
cloth, gilt. 10s. 6d. net.

ENGLISH COUNTRY LIFE AND WORK

An Account of some Past Aspects and Present Features. By ERNEST C.
PULBROOK. Containing about 200 pages on Farmers, Old and New—
Field-Work—Cottage Folk—The Village Craftsman—Religious Life, etc.
With about 200 artistic Illustrations from special Photographs. A New and
cheaper reissue. Large 8vo, cloth, gilt. 12s. 6d. net.

"We may congratulate the author on a very readable and well-illustrated book. He has
given a fairly detailed description of a large number of occupations of the English country
labourer and village dweller. . . . Such industries as thatching and hurdle-making are
described at some length, and there are good pages on country trading."—*The Field.*

OLD ENGLISH HOUSEHOLD LIFE

Some Account of Cottage Objects and Country Folk. By GERTRUDE
JEKYLL. Consisting of 17 sections on the Fireplace, Candlelight, the
Hearth, the Kitchen, Old Furniture, Home Industries, Cottage Buildings,
Itinerants, Mills, Churchyards, etc. With 277 Illustrations from Photo-
graphs and Old Prints and Drawings. New and cheaper reissue. Large
thick 8vo, cloth, gilt. 12s. 6d. net.

THE COTTAGES OF ENGLAND

A Regional Survey from the XVIth to the XVIIIth Century. By BASIL
OLIVER, F.R.I.B.A. The local types of every county are thoroughly represented in about 196 Photographic Illustrations, including 16 Plates in
Collotype, and the book forms the most thorough collection yet made of
these fine survivals of old English life. With a Frontispiece in colour and
a Foreword by the Rt. Hon. STANLEY BALDWIN, M.P. Large 8vo, cloth,
gilt, with decorative coloured wrapper. 21s. net.

TOURING ENGLAND BY ROAD AND BYWAY

A Popular Illustrated Guide in a new form to the Beauties of Rural England.
By SYDNEY R. JONES. Comprising 20 Typical Tours under Five Divisions,
with General Introduction and complete Map, Introduction to each
District and specially drawn simplified Route Map of each Tour, which is
described in detail, with finger-post reference to features, and buildings of
interest. Illustrated by 54 Drawings, including a number full page,
specially drawn by the Author, and 50 Illustrations from Photographs by
the Artist and others. New and cheaper issue. Crown 8vo, cloth. 5s. net.

"This little book is a delightful guide to the English countryside, useful alike to walker,
cyclist, and motorist."—*Queen.*

LITTLE KNOWN ENGLAND: RAMBLES IN THE WELSH BORDER-LAND, THE ROLLING UPLANDS, THE CHALK HILLS, AND THE EASTERN COUNTIES

By HAROLD DONALDSON EBERLEIN, Author of numerous works on Architecture, Decoration and Furniture. With about 120 Illustrations, 80 from Photographs and Paintings, and 40 in the text from Drawings, Sketches, Engravings, etc. Including a series of Maps. 8vo, cloth, lettered. 12s. 6d. net.

GEORGIAN ENGLAND (1700-1830)

A Review of its Social Life, Arts and Industries. By Professor A. E. RICHARDSON, F.S.A., F.R.I.B.A., Author of "The English Inn," etc. Containing sections on the Social Scene, Navy, Army, Church, Sport, Architecture, Building Crafts, the Trades, Decorative Arts, Painting, Literature, Theatres, etc. Illustrated by 200 subjects from Photographs and contemporary Prints, Engravings and Drawings, by Hogarth, Wheatley, Gainsborough, Reynolds, Rowlandson, and other artists. With 54 Line Text Illustrations, largely unpublished, and a Colour Frontispiece from an unpublished aquatint by ROBERT DIGHTON. Med. 8vo, cloth, gilt. 21s. net.

A TOUR THRO' LONDON ABOUT THE YEAR 1725

Being Letter V and parts of Letter VI of "A Tour Thro' the Whole Island of Great Britain." Containing a description of the City of London, taking in the City of Westminster, Borough of Southwark and Parts of Middlesex. By DANIEL DEFOE. Reprinted from the Original Edition (1724-1726). Edited and Annotated by SIR MAYSON BEETON, K.B.E., M.A., and E. BERESFORD CHANCELLOR, M.A., F.S.A. With Introduction, Prefatory Note, etc. Illustrated by 2 contemporary (end paper) and 4 specially drawn folding Maps and 56 full-page Plates, 16 hand-printed in Photogravure and the rest in Collotype, representing some 80 Buildings (many now vanished), Squares, Markets, Assemblies, the River, etc., from contemporary Prints, etc. Small folio, antique panelled, calf, gilt, gilt top. £11 11s. net; or in cloth, gilt, antique style, £8 8s. net.

Edition limited to 350 copies, of which but few remain for sale.

TOURING LONDON

By W. TEIGNMOUTH SHORE, Author of "Dinner Building," etc. With an Introduction by the Rt. Hon. JOHN BURNS, P.C. A Series of 4 Tours covering the chief parts of Inner London, written in a bright and pleasant style, but conveying much practical and historical information. Illustrated by 28 Photographs, with Drawings and Sketches in the text by well-known artists. Also a two-colour Map of the city, and Plans. Cheaper reissue. Large crown 8vo, cloth. 2s. 6d. net.

HISTORIC COSTUME

A Chronicle of Fashion in Western Europe, 1490-1790. By FRANCIS M. KELLY and RANDOLPH SCHWABE. Containing the chief characteristics of Dress in each century. Illustrated by some hundreds of full-page and text Sketches from original sources by RANDOLPH SCHWABE of typical groups, figures and details. Including 7 Plates specially reproduced in colour, and 70 Photographic reproductions of Historic Pictures, Portraits, Scenes, etc. Second Edition revised and enlarged. Large Royal 8vo, cloth, gilt, 25s. net.

"Intended primarily for the costumier, film producer, and artist, it is full of delight for the ordinary reader, who will find it an excellent help in the pleasant game of trying to construct a livelier vision of the past."—*The Queen.*

A SHORT HISTORY OF COSTUME AND ARMOUR, CHIEFLY IN ENGLAND, 1066-1800
By F. M. KELLY and RANDOLPH SCHWABE, Principal of the Slade School of Fine Art. Royal 8vo, cloth, gilt. 25s. net. Or in 2 volumes:
I. THE MIDDLE AGES, 1066-1485. With Sections on Civilian Dress: "Shirts," "Shapes," Houppelandes and Burgundian Modes; Armour. Illustrated by 4 Plates in colours and gold, over 100 special Pen Drawings by RANDOLPH SCHWABE from original sources and 32 Photographic Plates of over 70 reproductions. Royal 8vo, cloth, gilt. 13s. net.
II. THE RENAISSANCE, 1485-1800. With Sections on Puff and Slashes, The Spanish Trend, "Cavalier" and French Modes, the Heyday and Decline of Powder, Armour, etc. Illustrated by 5 Plates (3 double) in colours and gold, over 100 special Pen Drawings by RANDOLPH SCHWABE from original sources, 36 Photographic Plates of 58 Reproductions. Royal 8vo, cloth, gilt. 13s. net.

"Within its limits, it is undoubtedly the best book of its kind. Like their previous work, this present history is remarkable at once for its compression and its detail. The number of the illustrations alone is impressive, even more so is their quality. They make a picture-gallery of the past that will delight the ordinary reader almost as much as it will profit the student."—*Times Literary Supplement.*

MEDIAEVAL COSTUME AND LIFE
An Historic and Practical Review. By DOROTHY HARTLEY. Containing 22 full-page Plates from Photographs of living Male and Female Figures in specially made Costumes from Mediaeval MSS., 20 Plates in Line from the Author's Drawings of practical Construction, Detail, Sketches, etc., and 40 Plates of some 200 Reproductions from Contemporary Manuscripts of scenes of Mediæval life and work. Including full historical and descriptive text, with directions for the practical cutting out and making of many costumes illustrated. Large royal 8vo, cloth. 12s. net.

"Miss Hartley has treated the subject in a refreshingly original manner. She gives a great deal of practical advice, and the whole pageant of costume is linked up with society in such a way that we get a startlingly definite view of daily life and work. Altogether a fascinating handbook."—*Sunday Times.*

THE "PEOPLE'S LIFE AND WORK" SERIES
LIFE AND WORK OF THE ENGLISH PEOPLE THROUGH THE CENTURIES
A Pictorial Record from Contemporary Sources. By DOROTHY HARTLEY and MARGARET M. ELLIOT, B.A. (Lond.). Each volume is devoted to a separate century and contains 32 pp. of Text and about 150 pictures on 48 full-page Plates of Household Life, Crafts and Industries, Building, Farming, Warfare, City and Country Scenes, Transport, Children, Church Life, Gardens, etc. With an Introduction on the characteristics of each period, full Descriptive Notes, Historical Chart, Analytical Index, Music, etc. Large (royal) 8vo, boards, lettered, or in portfolio with flaps 3s. net per volume; or in cloth, 3s. 6d. net per volume. Volumes I and II (Early Middle Ages), III and IV (Later Middle Ages), and V and VI (Renaissance) are also bound together in cloth, 6s. net each, and volumes I, II and III (Middle Ages), and IV, V and VI (Renaissance) are also combined in cloth at 9s. net each. A few remaining copies of volumes II and III (Later Middle Ages), and volumes IV and V (Early and Middle Renaissance), can also be obtained bound together in cloth at 5s. net each.

The Series has now been completed as follows:

I. SAXON TIMES TO 1300   IV. THE SIXTEENTH CENTURY
II. THE FOURTEENTH CENTURY   V. THE SEVENTEENTH CENTURY
III. THE FIFTEENTH CENTURY   VI. THE EIGHTEENTH CENTURY

"A delightful collection of contemporary pictures largely taken from manuscripts. Of recent years we have had a bewildering output of picture-books, but we do not know of any on such a scale as this, cheap enough to find their way into the actual possession of children."—*The Manchester Guardian.*

The Quennell Series of Books on Social Life and History

"In their volumes the authors have covered history from the Old Stone Age to the Industrial Revolution. They have approached history from a new angle and in the process have revolutionised the teaching of it. In their hands it has become a live, vivid, and picturesque subject, for they have breathed new life into old bones. Their methods in narrative and illustration are now widely and generally recognised and appreciated." *Western Mail.*

A HISTORY OF EVERYDAY THINGS IN ENGLAND, 1066-1799

Written and Illustrated by MARJORIE and C. H. B. QUENNELL. In Two Volumes. Medium 8vo. 8s. 6d. net each; also issued bound in one volume, 16s. 6d. net.

This account of the English People in their everyday life, of their occupations and amusements during seven centuries, may be read with enjoyment by all interested in the life of Great Britain. The book appeals strongly to Students, Designers, and those interested in Buildings, Decoration, and Costume.

VOL. I.—EVERYDAY THINGS IN ENGLAND, 1066-1499

With 90 Illustrations, many full-page, and 3 Plates in colour. Second Edition, revised and enlarged, with additional illustrations.

VOL. II.—EVERYDAY THINGS IN ENGLAND, 1500-1799

By MARJORIE and C. H. B. QUENNELL. With 4 Coloured Plates and 111 other Illustrations from the Author's Drawings. Second Edition, revised and enlarged, with additional Illustrations.

Issued in Parts for Schools and Class Teaching

The work is now obtainable in Six Separate Parts, each covering a period of history of about a century, appropriate for a term's study. Each part has its own TITLE, CONTENTS, and FULL INDEX; the ILLUSTRATIONS are all given, and the coloured plates and comparative charts are also included. Bound in stiff paper covers (with the original special design), at 3s. net each part.

PART I. ENGLAND UNDER FOREIGN KINGS (1066-1199). Containing 2 Colour Plates, 5 full-page line Illustrations, and 15 in the text.

PART II. THE RISE OF PARLIAMENT (1200-1399). Containing 2 Colour Plates, 8 full-page Illustrations, and 22 in the text.

PART III. THE HUNDRED YEARS' WAR (1400-1499). Containing 1 Colour Plate, 11 full-page line Illustrations, and 13 in the text.

PART IV. THE AGE OF ADVENTURE (1500-1599). Containing 2 Colour Plates, 16 full-page line Illustrations, and 30 in the text.

PART V. THE CROWN'S BID FOR POWER (1600-1699). Containing 1 Colour Plate, 11 full-page line Illustrations, and 21 in the text.

PART VI. THE RISE OF MODERN ENGLAND (1700-1799). Containing 1 Colour Plate, 11 full-page line Illustrations, and 19 in the text.

VOL. III.—EVERYDAY THINGS IN ENGLAND, 1733-1851

THE COMING OF THE INDUSTRIAL ERA. An Account of the Transition from Traditional to Modern Life and Civilization. Written and Illustrated by MARJORIE and C. H. B. QUENNELL. Tracing the Transformation of Agriculture, the coming of Steam Power, the application of Inventions, Trends in Social Life in Town and Country, Costume, Building, etc. Illustrated by 4 Coloured Plates, 120 full-page and smaller Drawings specially prepared by the Authors, and a series of Reproductions of contemporary Engravings and Drawings. Medium 8vo, art canvas. 8s. 6d. net.

THE EVERYDAY LIFE SERIES

*A Graphic and Popular Survey of the Efforts and Progress of the Human Race,
now completed in 4 volumes. Crown 8vo. cloth. 5s. net. each.*

EVERYDAY LIFE IN THE OLD STONE AGE

Written and Illustrated by MARJORIE and C. H. B. QUENNELL. Containing
128 pages, including 70 Illustrations, and a coloured Frontispiece, from the
Authors' Drawings, with a Chronological Chart. Second Edition, revised.

"A small book containing much substance. . . . A vivid, simple style and sprightly
humour—which last is carried even into their clever black-and-white illustrations—should
give them many appreciative readers. A most attractive little book."—*The Morning Post.*

EVERYDAY LIFE IN THE NEW STONE, BRONZE AND EARLY IRON AGES

Written and Illustrated by MARJORIE and C. H. B. QUENNELL. Containing
144 pages, with 90 original Illustrations from the Authors' Drawings, of
Household Life, Agriculture, Pottery, Weapons, Ornaments, etc., including
2 Plates in colour, a marked Map, and a Chronological Chart. Second
Edition, revised.

*The above two works may now be obtained bound in one handy volume as described
below:*

EVERYDAY LIFE IN PREHISTORIC TIMES

Containing 272 pages, 3 Plates in colour and 2 in monochrome, with 160
Illustrations from the Authors' Pen-and-Ink Drawings, two Chronological
Charts and a Comparative Map. The Old Stone Age Section has an Account
of the Rhodesian Skull and Nebraskan Tooth, with 2 additional Illustrations.
Crown 8vo, cloth, lettered. 10s. net.

EVERYDAY LIFE IN ROMAN BRITAIN

Written and Illustrated by MARJORIE and C. H. B. QUENNELL. Containing
128 pages, with over 100 original Illustrations from the Authors' Pen
Drawings, of Cities and Camps, Villas, Ships, Chariots, Monuments, Costume, Military Life, Household Objects, Pottery, etc. Including 3 Colour
Plates, Chart, and Map of Roads.

EVERYDAY LIFE IN SAXON, VIKING, AND NORMAN TIMES

Written and Illustrated by MARJORIE and C. H. B. QUENNELL. Con-
taining 128 pages, with over 100 original Illustrations from the Authors'
Pen and Pencil Drawings of Ships, Cooking, Metalwork, Caskets, Crosses,
Buildings, Pottery, and Illuminated MSS., including 2 coloured Plates,
Historical Chart, etc. Crown 8vo, cloth. 5s. net.

"It is a period which gives scope for interesting writing and delightful illustrations. The
authors have, as before, profited to the full by their opportunities. Altogether this is an
agreeable as well as a valuable book, and one can say of the authors what Asser said of
Alfred. They are 'affable and pleasant to all, and curiously eager to   vestigate things
unknown.' "—*The Times.*

ENGLAND IN TUDOR TIMES

An Account of its Social Life and Industries. By L. F. SALZMAN, M.A.,
F.S.A., Author of "English Industries of the Middle Ages," etc. A remarkable survey of a great period in England's Social history. Containing
chapters on The Spirit of the Tudor Age—Life in the Country—Life in
the Town—Life in the Home—The Church—Adventure on Land and
Sea. With 138 pages of text, 64 full-page illustrations and plentiful illustrations in the text from Drawings, Engravings, etc. Cheaper reissue.
Demy 8vo., cloth. 5s. net.

A New Fascinating Series of Classical Social Life. Uniform with the Author's "Everyday Things in England."

EVERYDAY THINGS IN ANCIENT GREECE (HOMERIC—ARCHAIC—CLASSICAL)

An "Omnibus" Volume of the three following works. Written and Illustrated by MARJORIE and C. H. B. QUENNELL. A full review of Social Life and the Arts. Containing 3 coloured Plates, some 238 full-page and smaller Illustrations from Drawings in Pen-and-Ink, Pencil, and Wash and 20 from Photographs. Large thick 8vo. 21s. net.

VOL. I. EVERYDAY THINGS IN HOMERIC GREECE

Written and Illustrated by MARJORIE and C. H. B. QUENNELL, Authors of "The Everyday Life Series," etc. Presenting a vivid picture based on the Social Life in the Iliad and Odyssey, etc. Illustrated by about 70 full-page and smaller Drawings by the Authors, after early Vase Paintings and their own restorations. With Colour Frontispiece, Photographic Illustrations, Map, etc. Large 8vo, decoratively bound. 7s. 6d. net.

VOL. II. EVERYDAY THINGS IN ARCHAIC GREECE

Written and Illustrated by MARJORIE and C. H. B. QUENNELL. A Graphic Account of Social Life from the close of the Trojan War to the Persian Struggle, treating of Herodotus and his History, the Temple and the House, Life inside the House, and Life outside the House. Illustrated by 85 full-page and smaller Drawings by the Authors, specially prepared for the book· With a coloured Frontispiece, a number of Photographic Illustrations, Map, etc. Large 8vo, cloth, lettered. 7s. 6d. net.

"The Quennell books are likely to outlast some of the most imposing institutions of the post-war world. A book which is written with great scholarship and surprising lucidity. To speak in superlatives of this series is only justice, for seldom is there found such a unity between publisher, author, and illustrator as the Batsford books display."—*G.K.'s Weekly.*

VOL. III. EVERYDAY THINGS IN CLASSICAL GREECE

Written and Illustrated by MARJORIE and C. H. B. QUENNELL. A vivid picture of Social Life in the Golden Age of Pericles, Socrates, Phidias, Plato, and the building of the Parthenon, 480-404 B.C. With Sections on Architecture; The Town and its Planning; Town Houses and Everuday Life; Sea Fights and Land Battles, etc. Illustrated by 83 full-page and smaller Pen-and-Ink or Wash Drawings specially made by the Authors. With coloured Frontispiece, Series of Photographic Illustrations, Historical Chart, Map, etc. Large 8vo, cloth, lettered. 8s. net.

If ordered at one time the three volumes of this series are priced at 22s. net.

"ESSENTIALS OF LIFE" SERIES

By Lieut.-Colonel F. S. BRERETON, C.B.E. Bright, informative reviews of the Indispensable Things of Human Life. Each with 80 pages of text, and about 100 Illustrations in Line and Half-tone from Photographs, Drawings, Old Prints, etc., of Old and Modern Developments. Large crown 8vo, cloth, lettered. 4s. net each.

I. CLOTHING: An Account of its Types and Manufacture. Contents: Materials—Spinning—Weaving—The Sewing Machine—A Modern Factory—Furs and Rubber—Leather and Tanning—Boots—Hats—Glove-making—Dyeing and Cleaning—Pins—Needles—Buttons, etc.

II. TRAVEL: An Account of its Methods in Past and Present. Contents: Early Roads and Trading Routes—Coaching—The Steam Engine—Steamships and Railways—The Bicycle—The Petrol Engine—Air Travel—Postman—Wire or Wireless. With Illustrations of Coaches, Engines, Balloons, Aircraft, Ships, Steamers, etc.

"Each volume is illustrated with a wealth of pictures from old and modern sources. The text is written in an easy, discursive style that should popularise the books, and is yet packed with sound knowledge and fact."—*L'Atlantique.*

A HISTORY OF ARCHITECTURE ON THE COMPARA-
TIVE METHOD
For the Student, Craftsman, and Amateur.   By Sir BANISTER FLETCHER,
PP.R.I.B.A.   Eighth Edition, completely re-written.   Containing nearly
1000 pages, with about 3500 Illustrations (1560 recently added and nearly
2000 reproduced larger for this Edition), from Photographs and Drawings
of Buildings of all Countries and Times. Royal 8vo, cloth, gilt. £2 2s. net.

A SHORT CRITICAL HISTORY OF ARCHITECTURE
By H. HEATHCOTE STATHAM, F.R.I.B.A.   Second Edition, revised and
enlarged by G. MAXWELL AYLWIN, F.R.I.B.A.   Containing 600 pages
and 750 Illustrations from Photographs, Drawings, Plans, Prints, etc.,
with Chronological Charts and Glossary. Demy 8vo, cloth, gilt. 16s. net.
Also supplied in 3 parts, cloth, gilt. 6s. net each.
      I. ARCHITECTURE OF ANTIQUITY AND THE CLASSIC AGES.
     II. BYZANTINE, ROMANESQUE AND SARACENIC STYLES.
    III. THE MIDDLE AGES AND THE RENAISSANCE TO MODERN
         TIMES.
Eact part contains about 200 pages, with 250 full-page and smaller Illustrations, and is complete with Prefaces, Charts, Glossary and Indexes.
"Within the limits of its size and price it is the most valuable handbook that has
appeared in English for those who wish to understand the architecture of the past."
—*The Architect.*

THE STORY OF ARCHITECTURE
From the Earliest Ages to the Present Day.   By P. LESLIE WATERHOUSE,
F.R.I.B.A.   With Illustrations of the great buildings of all time from
Photographs and Drawings, and many Diagrams in the text. F'Cap 8vo,
boards, lettered. 6s. net.

THE STORY OF ARCHITECTURE IN ENGLAND
By WALTER H. GODFREY, F.S.A., F.R.I.B.A.   A popular illustrated account,
in which the aims and methods of Architectural Design are simply explained,
and linked up with the social life of the time. In Two Parts: I. Early and
Mediæval, to 1500, chiefly Churches; II. Renaissance, 1500-1800, chiefly
Houses. Demy 8vo, cloth. 6s. 6d. net per part; or the two volumes bound
in one, 12s. 6d. net.
I. PRE-REFORMATION, THE PERIOD OF CHURCH BUILDING
Illustrated by 133 full-page and smaller Photographs and Drawings. Large
crown 8vo, cloth. 6s. 6d. net.
II. RENAISSANCE, THE PERIOD OF HOUSE BUILDING
Illustrated by 150 full-page and smaller photographs and drawings. Large
crown 8vo, cloth, 6s. 6d. net.

*NEW EDITION REVISED AND ENLARGED NOW READY OF
THIS GREAT STANDARD WORK*
THE   DOMESTIC   ARCHITECTURE   OF   ENGLAND
DURING THE TUDOR PERIOD
Illustrated in a Series of Photographs and Measured Drawings of Country
Houses, Manor Houses and Other Buildings. By THOMAS GARNER and
ARTHUR STRATTON, F.R.I.B.A.   Second Edition, Revised and Enlarged,
comprising 210 Plates, mostly full page, finely reproduced in Collotype, and
250 pages of Historical and Descriptive Text, including 462 illustrations
of Additional Views, Plans, Details, etc., from photographs and drawings,
making a total of over 800 Illustrations in all. In two volumes, small folio,
buckram, gilt. £9 9s. net the set. (The volumes cannot be obtained
separately.)

BATSFORD'S
"HISTORICAL ARCHITECTURAL LIBRARY"
of Standard Textbooks on Classic and Renaissance Architecture.

BYZANTINE ARCHITECTURE AND DECORATION

By J. ARNOTT HAMILTON, M.A., author of "The Churches of Palermo,"
etc. A careful, scholarly and thorough account of the development and
character of constructional methods and decoration, and types of extant
buildings in Constantinople, Greece, the Balkans, Cyprus, Armenia,
Italy, etc. With 120 Photographic Illustrations of exteriors and interiors,
Reconstructions, Constructional Diagrams, Carving, Details, etc., and
numerous Line Plans, Measured Drawings, and Sketches in the text.
Medium 8vo, cloth, gilt. 18s. net.

ANDERSON AND SPIERS' "ARCHITECTURE OF GREECE AND ROME"

Now reissued in two volumes, obtainable separately, revised and much
enlarged. Small Royal 8vo, cloth, gilt. 21s. net each volume, or £2 the two.

I. ARCHITECTURE OF ANCIENT GREECE.   Re-written, Remodelled and much enlarged by WILLIAM BELL DINSMOOR, Professor
of Architecture at Columbia University, New York, and the American
Academy at Athens. With over 200 Illustrations in Collotype, half-tone
and line.

II. ARCHITECTURE OF ANCIENT ROME.   Revised and Re-
written by THOMAS ASHBY, Late Director of the British School at Rome.
With about 200 Illustrations in half-tone and line.

ARCHITECTURE OF THE RENAISSANCE IN ITALY

By WILLIAM J. ANDERSON, A.R.I.B.A. Revised and Enlarged, with an
additional Chapter on Baroque and Later work, by ARTHUR STRATTON,
F.S.A., F.R.I.B.A. With 80 Plates, including 16 in Collotype, and 120
Illustrations in the text. Small Royal 8vo, cloth, gilt. 21s. net.

ARCHITECTURE OF THE RENAISSANCE IN FRANCE

By W. H. WARD, M.A., F.R.I.B.A. Revised and Enlarged by Sir JOHN
W. SIMPSON, K.B.E., P.P.R.I.B.A. In two volumes, obtainable separately.
Small Royal 8vo, cloth, gilt. 21s. net, each volume, or £2 for the two.

IV. THE EARLY RENAISSANCE (1495-1640). With 259 Illustrations.
V. THE LATER RENAISSANCE (1640-1830). With 214 Illustrations.

RENAISSANCE PALACES OF NORTHERN ITALY

(With some Buildings of Earlier Periods). A General Review from the
XIIIth to the XVIIth Centuries. Revised and Edited by PROFESSOR DR.
ALBRECHT HAUPT. A Condensed Edition in 3 vols. of this Great Standard
Work, each containing 160 full-page Plates, reproduced in Collotype from
specially taken Photographs or from Measured Drawings expressly pre-
pared. With full historical and descriptive text.   Vol. I., TUSCANY,
FLORENCE, PISA, SIENA, MONTEPULCIANO, LUCCA, PISTOIA, etc.; Vol. II.,
VENICE, including also VERONA, MANTUA, VICENZA, and PADUA;
Vol. III., GENOA, including also BOLOGNA, FERRARA, MODENA, MILAN,
TURIN, PAVIA, BERGAMO, BRESCIA, etc. Small folio, cloth, lettered, £2 15s.
net each volume, or the set of 3 for £7 10s. net.

"One of the most welcome publications which has issued from the House of Batsford.
Their convenient size and excellent quality will appeal to those who are probably deterred
by the cost and large size of many fine architectural works. They will be a source of
continued delight and interest."—*The Builder.*

A NEW AND IMPORTANT SERIES OF SCHOOL WALL CHARTS
  *In Two Series now ready, consisting of 25 large lithographed Plates, 30 in. by
  20 in. Price Complete 25s. net on stout paper; or £3 2s. od. net mounted on linen,
  with bound edges. Single diagrams, 1s. 4d. net each; or mounted, 2s. 10d. net each.
  Introductory Handbook to each Series, 1s. 6d. net each, stiff paper covers, 2s. 6d.
  net each, cloth, lettered.*

THE STYLES OF ENGLISH ARCHITECTURE

A SERIES OF COMPARATIVE WALL OR LECTURE DIAGRAMS. For Schools,
Teachers, Students, etc. By ARTHUR STRATTON, F.S.A., F.R.I.B.A.
Series I.: THE MIDDLE AGES (Saxon Times to the Start of the Tudor
Period). Consisting of 13 large double crown Plates, 20 in. by 30 in.
clearly lithographed from the Author's specially prepared Drawings. 13s.
net paper, 32s. net mounted.
Series II: THE RENAISSANCE (Tudor, Elizabethan, Stuart, and Georgian
Periods). Comprising 12 large diagrams, as in Series I. 12s. net paper,
30s. net mounted.
The 32 pp. Introductory Handbooks contain reduced reproductions of all
the Plates with all their sources noted, and an outline account of each style
with numerous further Line Illustrations in the text.

ELEMENTS OF FORM AND DESIGN IN CLASSIC ARCHITECTURE

Shown in Exterior and Interior Motives collated from Fine Buildings of
all Times. By ARTHUR STRATTON, F.S.A., F.R.I.B.A. Presenting in 80 full-
page Plates about 600 motives of Façades, Loggias, Halls, Staircases, etc.
Including a Series of 16 Plates of Classic and Renaissance Compositions
and Designs. With Introduction, Analytical Account to each Section.
Descriptive Notes, and Foreword by Prof. A. E. RICHARDSON, F.S.A.,
F.R.I.B.A. 4to, cloth, gilt. 28s. net.

THE ORDERS OF ARCHITECTURE

GREEK, ROMAN, and RENAISSANCE; with EXAMPLES of their historic APPLI-
CATION IN ITALIAN, FRENCH, ENGLISH, and AMERICAN COLONIAL. By
ARTHUR STRATTON, F.S.A. With an Introduction by A. TRYSTAN EDWARDS,
A.R.I.B.A. Illustrated in a Series of 80 full-page Plates from Drawings,
mostly specially prepared, including a complete series of Vignola's Orders,
and rendered examples of French, Italian, and English buildings. With
full historical and practical notes and numerous Text Illustrations. 4to,
cloth, gilt, or in portfolio, 21s. net; or in 3 parts: CLASSIC, ITALIAN,
and APPLICATIONS, cloth 8s. net each.

THE ORDERS OF ARCHITECTURE

By R. PHENÉ SPIERS, F.S.A., F.R.I.B.A. A collection of typical Examples
of the Greek, Roman and Italian Orders selected from Normand's
"Parallels" and other Authorities, with Notes on Origin and Development
and descriptions of the Plates, Revised Bibliography, etc. Fifth Edition,
revised and enlarged, containing 27 full-page Plates. Large 4to, half-
cloth. 12s. 6d. net.
"An indispensable possession to all students of architecture."—*The Architect.*

ANCIENT ARCHITECTURE, PREHISTORIC, EGYPTIAN, WEST ASIAN, GREEK & ROMAN

A Chronicle in Verse, by H. CHESTER JONES, M.A., F.S.A. Comprising
also an outline history of Architecture, brief Prose Introductions to each
Section, and a full Glossary of Terms, etc. Illustrated by numerous large
Charts and Compositions and many Drawings and Plans of Buildings by
the Author. Including a photogravure portrait and appreciative Forewords
by Sir EDWIN LUTYENS, R.A., Dr. HADEN GUEST, M.P., and others. Large
8vo, cloth, gilt. 15s. net.

THE GROWTH OF THE ENGLISH HOUSE
A short History of its Design and Development from 1100 to 1800 A.D. By J. ALFRED GOTCH, F.S.A., PP.R.I.B.A. Containing 300 pages, with over 150 Illustrations from Photographs, and many pictures in the text from Measured Drawings, Sketches, Plans, and Old Prints. Second Edition, revised and enlarged. Large crown 8vo, cloth, gilt. 12s. 6d. net.

THE SMALLER ENGLISH HOUSE FROM THE RESTORATION TO THE VICTORIAN ERA, 1660-1840
By A. E. RICHARDSON, F.S.A., F.R.I.B.A., and HAROLD DONALDSON EBERLEIN, B.A. Treating of the Characteristics and Periods of Style; the Evolution of Plan; Materials and Craftsmanship: Roofing, Windows, Ironwork, Fireplaces, Staircases, Wall Treatment, Ceilings. With over 200 Illustrations, many full page, from Photographs and Drawings. Demy 4to, cloth, gilt. Cheaper reissue, 15s. net.

ENGLISH GOTHIC CHURCHES
THE STORY OF THEIR ARCHITECTURE. By CHARLES W. BUDDEN, M.A. A simple, informative account of the Planning, Design, and Details of Parish Churches, Cathedrals, etc., 1066-1500, including Chapters on Local Building, Towers, Spires, Ornaments, etc. Illustrated by 53 Plans and Line Diagrams, and 40 Photographic Plates of 80 Views and Details, including a County List of the chief Churches worth seeing. Crown 8vo, cloth, cheaper reissue, 5s. net.

THE "COUNTY CHURCH" SERIES
Edited by the Rev. J. C. Cox, LL.D., F.S.A. Twelve volumes, each containing numerous Plates from Photographs, and Illustrations from Drawings in the text. F'Cap 8vo, cloth, gilt. 2s. 6d. net per volume.
CAMBRIDGESHIRE AND THE ISLE OF ELY. By C. H. EVELYN-WHITE, F.S.A.
CORNWALL. By J. C. Cox, LL.D., F.S.A.
CUMBERLAND AND WESTMORLAND. By J. C. Cox, LL.D., F.S.A.
ISLE OF WIGHT. By J. C. Cox, LL.D., F.S.A.
KENT (2 Vols. sold separately). By F. GRAYLING.
NORFOLK (2 Vols.). Second Edition, revised and extended. By J. C. Cox, LL.D., F.S.A. (*Now out of print.*)
NOTTINGHAMSHIRE. By J. C. Cox, LL.D., F.S.A.
SURREY. By J. E. MORRIS, B.A.
SUFFOLK (2 Vols. sold separately). By T. H. BRYANT.

OLD CROSSES AND LYCHGATES
A Study of their Design and Craftsmanship. By AYMER VALLANCE, M.A., F.S.A. With over 200 fine Illustrations from specially taken Photographs, Old Prints, and Drawings. Crown 4to, art linen. Cheaper reissue 12s. 6d. net.

ENGLISH CHURCH WOODWORK AND FURNITURE
A Study in Craftsmanship from A.D. 1250-1550. By F. E. HOWARD and F. H. CROSSLEY, F.S.A. Illustrating, in over 480 examples from Photographs, the Development of Screens, Stalls, Benches, Font-Covers, Roofs, Doors, Porches, etc., with details of the Carved and Painted Decoration, etc., etc. Second and cheaper Edition, revised, with a new series of 16 Collotype Plates. Crown 4to, cloth, gilt. 25s. net.

"As a treasury of examples, a large proportion of them almost unknown, and as a compendium of information and research, it is a possession of special interest and value. . . ."—*The Times Literary Supplement.*

ENGLISH CHURCH FITTINGS AND FURNITURE

By the Rev. J. C. Cox, LL.D., F.S.A. A Popular Survey, treating of Churchyards, Bells, Fonts and Covers, Pulpits, Lecterns, Screens, Chained Books,
Stained Glass, Organs, Plate and other features of interest. With upwards
of 250 Illustrations from Photographs and Drawings. 8vo, cloth, gilt.
New and cheaper reissue. 12s. 6d. net.

ENGLISH CHURCH MONUMENTS, A.D. 1150-1550

By F. H. Crossley, F.S.A. A survey of the work of the old English craftsmen in stone, marble, and alabaster. Containing over 250 pages, with
upwards of 350 Illustrations, from special Photographs and Drawings.
Crown 4to, cloth, gilt. Cheaper reissue 21s. net.

ENGLISH MURAL MONUMENTS AND TOMBSTONES

A Collection of Eighty-four Full-page Photographic Plates of Wall Tablets, Table Tombs, and Headstones of the Seventeenth and Eighteenth
Centuries, specially selected by Herbert Batsford for the use of Craftsmen. With an Introduction by W. H. Godfrey, F.S.A. Crown 4to, cloth,
gilt. 15s. net.

ANCIENT CHURCH CHESTS AND CHAIRS IN THE HOME COUNTIES ROUND GREATER LONDON

With some Reference to their Surroundings. By Fred Roe, R.I., R.B.C.
With a Foreword by C. Reginald Grundy. A survey of the finest of these
survivals of ancient craftsmanship by the leading authority on the subject.
With 95 Illustrations, many full page, from Drawings by the Author and
from Photographs, and a number of Line Illustrations in the text. Cheaper
reissue. Demy 4to, cloth, gilt. 12s. 6d. net.

EARLY CHURCH ART IN NORTHERN EUROPE

With special Reference to Timber Construction and Decoration. By
Josef Strzygowski, Author of "Origin of Christian Church Art," etc.
Dealing with Pre-Romanesque Art of the Croatians; Wooden Archi-
tecture in Eastern Europe; Half-Timber Churches in Western
Europe; The Mast Churches of Norway; Royal Tombs in Scandinavia.
With 190 Illustrations. Royal 8vo, cloth, gilt. 21s. net.

"Present-day writers on architecture cannot be said to be exactly exciting ; but Prof.
Strzygowski is the exception. For vigour and vehemence he is unsurpassed. A remarkable
book, with very much to study in it, if not always to convince."—The Dean of Winchester in *The Sunday Times.*

ENGLISH RENAISSANCE WOODWORK, 1660-1730

A Selection of the finest examples, monumental and domestic, chiefly of
the Period of Sir Christopher Wren. By Thomas J. Beveridge. A Series
of 80 fine Plates from the Author's measured drawings, specially prepared
and fully detailed, including Monographs on St. Paul's Choir Stalls, Hampton Court, Oxford and Cambridge Colleges, London City Churches, etc.
Including a series of Collotype Plates from pencil drawings, and illustrated
descriptive text. Large folio, half-bound, £3 net (originally published at
£6 6s. net).

ENGLISH LEADWORK: ITS ART AND HISTORY

A Book for Architects, Antiquaries, Craftsmen, and Owners and Lovers of
Gardens. By Sir Lawrence Weaver, F.S.A. Containing 280 pages, with
441 Illustrations from Photographs and Drawings. Large 4to, art linen,
gilt. 30s. net.

ENGLISH INTERIORS FROM SMALLER HOUSES OF THE XVIITH TO XIXTH CENTURIES, 1660-1820

By M. JOURDAIN. Illustrating the simpler type of Design during the Stuart, Georgian, and Regency Periods. Containing 200 pages, and 100 Plates, comprising 200 Illustrations, from Photographs and Measured Drawings of Interiors, Chimney-pieces, Staircases, Doors, Ceilings, Panelling, Metalwork, Carving, etc., from minor Country and Town Houses. With Introduction and Historical Notes. Cheaper reissue. Large 4to, cloth, gilt. 15s. net.

OLD ENGLISH FURNITURE FOR THE SMALL COLLECTOR

Its History, Types and Surroundings from Mediæval to Early Victorian Times. By J. P. BLAKE and A. E. REVEIRS-HOPKINS. Containing 150 pages with about 130 Illustrations from Photographs, Old Prints and Pictures, Original Designs, Ornaments, etc. The book is planned as the first systematic and comprehensive guide to the simpler types of old furniture within the scope of the collector of average means. Med. 8vo. 12s. 6d. net.

OLD ENGLISH FURNITURE : THE OAK PERIOD, 1550-1630

Its Characteristics, Features, and Detail from Tudor Times to the Regency. For the use of Collectors, Designers, Students, and Others. By J. T. GARSIDE. Containing 30 Plates reproduced from the Author's specially prepared Drawings illustrating about 400 details of Table Legs; Bed-posts; Corbels; Friezes; Capitals; Panels; Inlay Motives; Metal Fittings, etc. Including also Drawings of type-pieces of the period and 20 Photographic Illustrations. With an Historical Introduction, etc. Cheaper reissue. 8vo, cloth, gilt. 7s. 6d. net.

FRENCH FURNITURE AND DECORATION OF THE LOUIS XIV AND REGENCY STYLES

A Pictorial review of their chief Types and Features in the Late XVIIth and early XVIIIth Centuries. By CORRADO RICCI. Comprising 414 Illustrations, mostly from Photographs of various types of Interiors, Galleries, Halls, with characteristic specimens of Chairs, Tables, Bureaux, Settees, Cabinets, Beds, Mirrors, Stools, etc. With brief Introductory Text, illustrated by reproductions of Designs, by Lepautre, Berain, Marot, Watteau and others. 4to, cloth, gilt. 38s. net.

OLD SILVER OF EUROPE AND AMERICA

From Early Times to the XIXth Century. By E. ALFRED JONES. A Survey of the Old Silver of England, America, Austria, Belgium, Canada, Czecho-Slovakia, Denmark, France, Germany, Holland, Hungary, Ireland, Italy, Norway, Poland, Portugal, Russia, Scotland, Spain, Sweden, Switzerland, etc. With a Chapter on Spurious Plate and 96 Photogravure Plates, comprising Illustrations of 537 subjects. Cheaper reissue. Crown 4to, art canvas, lettered in silver. 18s. net.

EIGHTEENTH-CENTURY ARCHITECTURE IN SOUTH AFRICA

By Professor G. E. PEARSE, F.R.I B.A., Witwatersrand University, Johannesburg. With 130 Collotype Plates, from Photographs and specially prepared Measured Drawings of Country and Town Buildings and their Features, showing Views, Elevations, Plans, Interiors, Carving, Gardens, etc. With full Text, illustrated by Sketches, Engravings, etc. *Large 4to, buckram, gilt. £2 10s. net. Edition strictly limited to 500 copies. The subscription price may be raised as the small number becomes nearly exhausted.*

THE FOUR VOLUMES OF
BATSFORD'S LIBRARY OF DECORATIVE ART

form an attractive Series of remarkable scope and completeness. It reviews
the Development of English Decoration and Furniture during the three
Renaissance Centuries, XVI, XVII, and XVIII (1500-1820). Each volume
has an extensive series of Plates, and is a complete guide to the work of its
Period. The volumes are remarkable for the beauty and number of their
illustrations, the simplicity and clearness of their arrangement, and their
moderate prices. The complete series is published at prices amounting to
£10, but is supplied for the present at the special price of £9 net.

"These handsome volumes with their extremely fine and copious illustrations provide a
full survey of English Furniture and Decoration."—*The Times.*

VOL. I. DECORATION AND FURNITURE IN ENGLAND DURING THE EARLY RENAISSANCE, 1500-1660

An Account of their Development and Characteristic Forms during the
Tudor, Elizabethan and Jacobean Periods, by M. JOURDAIN. Containing
about 300 pages, and over 200 full-page Plates (with Coloured Frontispiece
and some in photogravure), including over 400 Illustrations, from specially
made Photographs and Measured Drawings, and from Engravings. Folio
(size 14 x 10½ in.), cloth, gilt. £2 10s. net.

VOL. II. FURNITURE IN ENGLAND FROM 1660 to 1760

By FRANCIS LENGYON. A Survey of the Development of its Chief Types.
Containing 300 pages with over 400 Illustrations, from special Photographs, together with 5 in colour. Second Edition, revised with many
new Illustrations. Folio (14 in. x 10½ in.), cloth, gilt. £2 10s. net.

VOL. III. DECORATION IN ENGLAND FROM 1640 to 1770

By FRANCIS LENGYON. A Review of its Development and Features. Containing 300 pages with over 350 Illustrations, of which 133 are full-page,
from special Photographs, and 4 in colour. Second Edition, Revised
and Enlarged. Folio (14 in. x 10½ in.), cloth, gilt. £2 10s. net.

VOL. IV. DECORATION AND FURNITURE IN ENGLAND DURING THE LATER XVIIITH CENTURY, 1760-1820

An Account of their Development and Characteristic Forms, by M. JOUR-
DAIN. Containing about 300 pages, with over 180 full-page Plates (a selection in Collotype), including over 400 Illustrations, from specially made
Photographs and Measured Drawings, and from Engravings. Folio
(size 14 x 10½ in.), cloth, gilt. £2 10s. net.

HISTORIC INTERIORS IN COLOUR

Illustrated in a Series of 80 full-page Plates, reproduced in facsimile from
Water-colours by well-known artists of Rooms of the later XVIIth to the
early XIXth Centuries, in Baroque, Rococo, Louis XVI, and Empire Styles,
in various Castles and private Houses in Germany, Austria, and France.
Comprising Salons, Dining-rooms, Ante-rooms, Music Rooms, Cabinets,
Bedrooms, Libraries, etc. With brief Text by A. Feulner. 4to, cloth, gilt.
40s. net.

A limited Edition of the first work on a fine, unknown Craft.

DOMESTIC UTENSILS OF WOOD

From the XVIth to the Mid-XIXth Century in England and on the
Continent. By OWEN EVAN-THOMAS. Illustrated by 70 full-page Plates
from specially arranged Photographs of 1000 subjects in the Author's
personal collection. Including full Introductory, Historical and Descriptive
Text. Large 4to, cloth, gilt. 21s. net.

THE LEVERHULME ART MONOGRAPHS

A Series of three sumptuous Volumes, folio, handsomely bound in art buckram, gilt. Price £15 15s. the set (volumes not sold separately). Edition strictly limited to 350 copies for sale, of which very few remain.

I. ENGLISH PAINTING OF THE XVIIIth AND XIXth CENTURIES

With some Examples of the Spanish, French, and Dutch Schools, and a Collection of Original Drawings and of Sculpture. By R. R. TATLOCK. Editor of the *Burlington Magazine*. With an Introduction by ROGER FRY. Containing 200 pages of Text, including Introductory Notes, and detailed Accounts of 1000 Pictures, Drawings, etc. Illustrated by 101 Photographic full-page Plates and 12 in Photogravure.

II. CHINESE PORCELAIN AND WEDGWOOD POTTERY

With other works of Ceramic Art. By R. L. HOBSON, B.A., British Museum. Containing 200 pages of Text, including Introductions and detailed descriptions of over 2000 Pieces. With over 75 Photographic Plates, and 30 Plates reproduced in colour.

III. ENGLISH FURNITURE, TAPESTRY, AND NEEDLE-WORK OF THE XVIth-XIXth CENTURIES

With some Examples of Foreign Styles. By PERCY MACQUOID, R.I. Containing 150 pages of Text, with Introductions and detailed descriptions of over 700 Objects. Illustrated by 104 Photographic Plates, and 9 Plates in full colour.

The three fine volumes which the late Viscount Leverhulme planned as a memorial to his wife constitute a record of his own permanent collections. Only 350 sets can be offered for subscription, and the very moderate figure of £15 15s. represents but a fraction of the immense expenses undertaken by Viscount Leverhulme.

CHILDREN'S TOYS OF BYGONE DAYS

A History of Playthings of all Peoples from Prehistoric Times to the XIXth Century. By KARL GRÖBER. English Version by PHILIP HEREFORD. A beautifully produced survey, with a frontispiece and 11 Plates in colour, and 306 photographic illustrations of Dolls, Dolls-houses, Mechanical Toys, Carts, Ships, Tin Soldiers, etc., etc., of every country and period from the earliest times. With 66 pages of historical and descriptive text. 4to, canvas, gilt, with decorative wrapper. New and cheaper edition, 12s. 6d. net.

"Its abundance of illustrations is wonderful. Many of them are in colour, and all are reproduced in a fashion which does the publishers credit. The text is as interesting as the pictures. We can heartily recommend this book to the public. No one who buys it will be disappointed."—*The Daily Mail.*

An Attractive Account of a little-known XVIIIth Century Craftsman. Dedicated by gracious permission to Her Majesty Queen Mary.

JOHN OBRISSET

Huguenot, Carver, Medallist, Horn and Tortoise-shell Worker, and Snuff-box Maker. With examples of his Works dated 1705-1728. By PHILIP A. S. PHILLIPS. Containing Text on the Records of the Obrisset family, Writings on his Craftsmanship and Notes. With 104 Illustrations on 40 Plates, finely reproduced in Collotype, of Horn and Tortoise-shell Tobacco-boxes, Medals, Plaques in different Materials, Medallions, etc. Edition limited to 250 numbered copies, of which 210 are for sale. 4to, canvas, gilt, gilt top. £3 3s. net.

BATSFORD'S COLLECTORS' LIBRARY

A Series of Handbooks written by experts, providing information of practical value to Connoisseurs, Collectors, Designers, and Students. Each volume forms an ideal introduction to its subject, and is fully illustrated by Reproductions in Colour and from Photographs. The following volumes are still available. 8vo, cloth, gilt, price 6s. net each.

*OLD ENGLISH FURNITURE. By F. FENN and B. WYLLIE. With 94 Illustrations. *New Impression.*

OLD PEWTER. By MALCOLM BELL. With 106 Illustrations.

SHEFFIELD PLATE. By BERTIE WYLLIE. With 121 Illustrations.

FRENCH FURNITURE. By ANDRE SAGLIO. With 59 Illustrations.

DUTCH POTTERY AND PORCELAIN. By W. P. KNOWLES. With 54 Illustrations.

*PORCELAIN. By WILLIAM BURTON. With over 50 full-page Plates illustrating 87 fine examples of the Porcelain of Various Countries and Periods.

OLD PEWTER : ITS MAKERS AND MARKS

A Guide for Collectors, Connoisseurs, and Antiquaries. By HOWARD HERSCHEL COTTERELL, First Vice-President of the Society of Pewter Collectors. Containing about 500 pages, with 64 Plates of 200 Specimens of British Pewter, dated and described, and a List of 5000 to 6000 Pewterers, with Illustrations of their Touches and Secondary Marks, Facsimile Reproductions of existing Touch-Plates, and Text Illustrations. Cheaper reissue. Demy 4to, cloth, gilt. £3 3s. net.

"Messrs. Batsford's work as publishers is of their usual high standard, and Mr. Cotterell has enhanced his already great reputation as an authority, and is to be congratulated on this ideal standard work which will perforce be the last word on the subject for many years to come."—*The Queen.*

AN ILLUSTRATED HISTORY OF ENGLISH PLATE

Ecclesiastical and Secular, illustrating the Development of Silver and Gold Work of the British Isles from the earliest known examples to the latest of the Georgian Period. By Sir CHARLES JAMES JACKSON, F.S.A. With a Coloured Frontispiece, 76 Plates finely executed in Photogravure, and 1500 other Illustrations, chiefly from Photographs. Two volumes, small folio, bound in half-morocco. £10 10s. net.

A HISTORY OF ENGLISH WALLPAPER

From the earliest Period to 1914. By A. V. SUGDEN and J. L. EDMONDSON. Comprising 270 pages on Wallpapers' ancestry—Early Wallpapers—Eighteenth Century Developments—Famous Pioneers—Chinese Papers and English Imitations—Late Georgian Achievements—The Coming of Machinery—How Wallpaper "found itself"—The Coming of William Morris—Developments of Taste and Technique—Mill Records. With 70 Plates in colour and 190 Illustrations in half-tone. Large 4to. handsome art buckram, gilt, boxed. £3 3s. net.

OLD AND CURIOUS PLAYING CARDS

Their History and Types from many Countries and Periods. By H. T. MORLEY, B.Sc. (Arch.), F.R.Hist.S. With a Foreword by Sidney Lambert. Past-Master of the Company of Makers of Playing Cards. Containing Chapters on History, Asiatic, European and English Cards (including Caricature, Astrology, Heraldry, etc.), Musical Cards, Games, etc. With over 330 Illustrations, many in colour. Crown 4to, canvas, lettered, cloth sides. 21s. net; or handsomely bound in leather, 30s. net.

A HISTORY OF BRITISH WATER-COLOUR PAINTING

By H. M. CUNDALL, F.S.A. With a Foreword by Sir H. HUGHES-STANTON, P.R.W.S. A New and Cheaper Edition, revised and enlarged, of this important standard work, with 64 full-page Illustrations in colour, and a full biographical list, arranged alphabetically, of the principal English Water-colourists. Large Medium 8vo, cloth, 15s. net.

"Apart from its value as a complete and authoritative work of reference in its specia subject the book forms a delightful picture gallery of the best British work in water-colours. The topographical and travel interest of the pictures reproduced has a wide range."—*Illustrated London News.*

THE BURLINGTON MAGAZINE MONOGRAPHS
Issued by the Publishers jointly with The Burlington Magazine

MONOGRAPH NO. I—CHINESE ART (*Out of print*)

MONOGRAPH NO. II—SPANISH ART

An Introductory Review of Architecture, Painting, Sculpture, Textiles, Ceramics, Woodwork, Metalwork, by ROYALL TYLER, Sir CHARLES HOLMES and H. ISHERWOOD KAY, GEOFFREY WEBB, A. F. KENDRICK, B. RACKHAM and A. VAN DE PUT, BERNARD BEVAN, and P. DE ARTINANO, respectively. With a General Introduction by R. R. TATLOCK, Editor of *The Burlington Magazine*. Illustrated by 120 large scale reproductions of Paintings, Decorative Art, Buildings, etc., including 9 Plates in full colour, comprising 280 pictures in all. With Maps, Bibliography, etc. Royal 4to, cloth. Cheaper reissue, 25s. net.

MONOGRAPH NO. III—GEORGIAN ART

A Survey of Art in England during the reign of George III, 1760-1820, by leading authorities. The Sections comprise: *Painting* by J. B. MANSON; *Architecture and Sculpture* by GEOFFREY WEBB; *Ceramics* by BERNARD RACKHAM; *Woodwork* by OLIVER BRACKETT; *Textiles* by A. F. KENDRICK; *Minor Arts* by LOUISE GORDON-STABLES. With an Introduction by ROGER FRY. The Illustrations include 6 Plates in colour and 64 in half-tone, comprising some 100 subjects, and forming a gallery of the fine and decorative arts of the Period. Cheaper reissue. Royal 4to, cloth, 21s. net.

"This large volume gives an authoritative survey of the arts enumerated, and the quality of the reproductions maintains the high standard associated with its source. The high reputation of the associated authors and the beauty of the illustrations combine to render the book an ideal fulfilment of its purpose."—*Illustrated London News.*

THE DECORATIVE ARTS IN ENGLAND, 1660-1780

By H. H. MULLINER, with an Introduction by J. STARKIE GARDNER. A Series of 110 full-page Plates from Photographs illustrating 256 Specimens of Furniture, Lacquering, Marquetry, and Gesso, Chandeliers, Clocks; Stuart and Georgian Silver—Sconces, Cups, Bowls, Tea and Coffee Sets—Enamels, Locks, Battersea Enamel, Ormolu Vases, Tapestry, Needlework, Bookbindings. With brief Historical Introductions and full descriptions. Folio, half-parchment, gilt. £3 10s. net.

ENGLISH PLASTERWORK OF THE RENAISSANCE

A Review of its Design during the Period from 1500 to 1800. By M. JOURDAIN. Comprising over 100 full-page Plates of Elizabethan, Stuart, Georgian, and Adam ceilings, friezes, overmentels, panels, ornament, detail, etc., from specially taken Photographs and from Measured Drawings and Sketches. With an Illustrated Historical Survey on Foreign Influences and the Evolution of Design, Work and Names of Craftsmen, etc. New and cheaper reissue. Demy 4to, cloth. 15s. net.

THE EARLY FLEMISH PAINTINGS IN THE RENDERS COLLECTION

Exhibited at the Flemish Exhibition, Burlington House. With a full Introduction by G. HULIN DE LOO, and detailed Descriptions of the Paintings by E. MICHEL. Containing 6 Mounted Plates in full colour, and 18 Plates in Photogravure of Paintings in the Collection of M. Renders of Bruges, including works by Rogier van der Weyden, Memling, Jean Provost, Mabuse, the Masters of S. Veronica and of the Baroncelli Portraits, etc., etc. Large 4to, the few remaining copies offered in portfolio, £1 1s. net; or bound in cloth, gilt, £1 5s. net.

"With the book in his hands he would be a dull reader indeed who cannot in a comparatively short time familiarise himself with several distinct aspects of the history of Flemish painting."—*The Daily Telegraph.*

THE XVIIITH CENTURY IN LONDON

An Account of its Social Life and Arts. By E. BERESFORD CHANCELLOR. Containing 280 pages, with 192 Illustrations, printed in sepia, from Prints and Drawings by contemporary artists. With a Frontispiece in colour. Cheaper reissue. Crown 4to, cloth, gilt. 15s. net.

A Companion and Sequel to the above

LIFE IN REGENCY AND EARLY VICTORIAN TIMES

An Account of Social Life in the days of Brummel and D'Orsay. By E. BERESFORD CHANCELLOR. A Series of Chapters on the time of Brummel and D'Orsay, 1800-1843. With numerous Illustrations from Rare Prints and Original Drawings. Cheaper reissue. Large 8vo, cloth, gilt. 12s. 6d. net.

THE ART AND CRAFT OF GARDEN MAKING

By THOMAS H. MAWSON, assisted by E. PRENTICE MAWSON. Fifth Edition, Revised and Enlarged. Containing 440 pages, illustrated by 544 Plans, Sketches, and Photographs, and 5 colour Plates. Including Site, Entrances, Gates, Avenues, Terraces, Beds, Pergolas, Treillage, Rock and Water, Greenhouses, etc., etc., and list of Shrubs and Trees. Small folio, buckram, gilt. £3 15s. net.

GARDENS IN THE MAKING

By WALTER H. GODFREY. A simple Guide to the Planning of a Garden. With upwards of 70 Illustrations of Plans, Views, and various Garden Accessories. Crown 8vo, cloth. 7s. 6d. net.

SPANISH GARDENS

By Mrs. C. M. VILLIERS-STUART. A finely illustrated volume describing the beautiful and most famous gardens of Spain, by one of the foremost authorities on the subject. With 6 Plates in colour from the Author's original Water-colour Drawings, 80 pages of reproductions of gardens, statuary, cascades, garden features, etc., from Photographs, and numerous Illustrations in the text from old Engravings, Pen Drawings, etc. Small royal 8vo, cloth. 25s. net.

"All who love beautiful illustrated books and all who are interested in gardens will do well to buy this delightful volume. The plates in colours from the author's water-colour drawings are exquisite. This book is one of the most attractive we have seen."—*Daily Mail*

LITTLE KNOWN TOWNS OF SPAIN

A series of Water-colours and Drawings in facsimile colour and monochrome from the originals of VERNON HOWE BAILEY. Comprising 57 full-page Plates, many in colour, others in sepia, wash, lithography, etc., with text, including historical and descriptive short notes. Large 4to, in decorative paper binding, £1 10s. net.

ART IN THE LIFE OF MANKIND

A Survey of its Achievements from the Earliest Times. By ALLEN W. SEABY. Planned in a series of concise volumes, each containing about 80 pages of text ,with about 70 full-page and smaller Illustrations from the author's specially prepared Sketches and Drawings, and a series of 16 Photographic Plates. Crown 8vo, cloth, 5s. net per volume. I. A GENERAL VIEW OF ART: ITS NATURE, MEANING, PRINCIPLES AND APPRECIATION. II. ANCIENT TIMES: THE ART OF ANCIENT EGYPT, CHALDÆA, ASSYRIA, PERSIA, and other lands. III. GREEK ART & ITS INFLUENCE. IV. ROMAN & BYZANTINE ART & THEIR INFLUENCE. Other volumes on Art.

These concise little volumes are designed to serve as an Introduction to the Appreciation and Study of Art in general. They are simply and graphically written and fully illustrated by many Drawings and Photographs.

A SHORT HISTORY OF ART

From Prehistoric times to the Nineteenth Century. Translated from the French of Dr. ANDRÉ BLUM. Edited and Revised by R. R. TATLOCK. Illustrated by 128 full-page Photographic Plates, comprising about 250 examples of the finest Painting, Sculpture, Architecture, and Decorative Art of Early, Classic, Byzantine, Gothic, Renaissance, and Recent Times. Including also about 100 Illustrations in the text from Drawings, Engravings, and Plans. Medium 8vo, cloth, gilt. 12s. 6d. net.

HISTORY OF ART

By JOSEPH PIJOAN, Professor at Pomona College, California. In 3 volumes, Royal 8vo, bound in cloth, gilt. 36s. net per volume (obtainable separately).

VOL. I. PRIMITIVE, ANCIENT AND CLASSIC ART. With 61 full-page Plates, including many in colour, and 876 Illustrations from Photographs, Plans, Drawings, Restorations, etc.

VOL. II. BYZANTINE, ISLAMIC, ROMANESQUE AND GOTHIC ART. With 52 double- and full-page Plates, including many in colour, and 856 Illustrations from Photographs, etc.

VOL. III. THE RENAISSANCE TO MODERN TIMES. With 34 full-page Plates, including many in colour and 776 Illustrations from Photographs, etc.

OLD MASTER DRAWINGS

A Quarterly Magazine, edited by K. T. PARKER, British Museum. With an Executive Committee of: CAMPBELL DODGSON, A. P. OPPÉ, M. HIND, and A. G. B. RUSSELL, and Consultative Foreign Authorities. Each number contains 16-20 Plates, and about 12 letterpress pages of articles and shorter notices dealing with Drawings from the earliest times to the 19th Century. Demy 4to. Annual subscription, 21s. net, post free; Single Numbers, 5s. 6d. net, post free.

No periodical devoted exclusively to the study and criticism of drawings has hitherto existed; this publication is intended to meet the need. The names of the many scholars connected with it guarantee its authoritative character, and its volumes are a mine of reference to students of art.

THE DRAWINGS OF ANTOINE WATTEAU, 1684-1721

By Dr. K. T. PARKER, of the British Museum, an Editor of "Old Master Drawings." A full, original and critical Survey. Illustrated by 100 Collotype Reproductions of selected characteristic Drawings from private and public collections, many unpublished, a Frontispiece in colour and 16 of the Master's most important pictures. With full, critical and descriptive letterpress. 4to, canvas cloth, gilt. £2 2s. net.

A MANUAL OF HISTORIC ORNAMENT
Being an Account of the Development of Architecture and the Historic Arts, for the use of Students and Craftsmen. By RICHARD GLAZIER, A.R.I.B.A. Fifth Edition, revised and enlarged. Containing 700 Illustrations, chiefly from the Author's Pen Drawings, including many new to this Edition from various sources, and a special series of Photographic Plates of Ornament of the Orient and the Renaissance. Large 8vo, cloth. 12s. 6d. net.

"The result of revision is admirable in every respect : the book is immensely improved, and its scope considerably broadened, though it is still compact and easy of reference. It is now the ideal manual for the student or craftsman, and those who are wise enough to purchase it will possess not only an invaluable work of reference, but a source of inspiration as well."—*The Decorator.*

A HANDBOOK OF ORNAMENT
With 3000 Illustrations of the Elements and the Application of Decoration to Objects, e.g., Vases, Frets, Diapers, Consoles, Frames, Jewellery, Heraldry, etc., grouped on over 300 Plates, reproduced from the Author's specially prepared Drawings. With descriptive text to each subject. By Professor F. SALES MEYER. Large 8vo, cloth, lettered. 16s. net.

"IT IS A LIBRARY, A MUSEUM, AN ENCYCLOPÆDIA, AND AN ART SCHOOL IN ONE. To RIVAL IT AS A BOOK OF REFERENCE ONE MUST FILL A BOOKCASE. The quality of the drawings is unusually high, and the choice of examples is singularly good. . . . The text is well digested, and not merely descriptive or didactic, but an admirable mixture of example and precept. So good a book needs no praise."—*The Studio.*

THE STYLES OF ORNAMENT
From Prehistoric Times to the Middle of the XIXth Century. A Series of 3500 Examples Arranged in Historical Order, with descriptive text. By ALEXANDER SPELTZ. Revised and Edited by R. PHENÉ SPIERS, F.S.A., F.R.I.B.A. Containing 560 pages, with 400 full-page Plates exhibiting upwards of 3500 separate Illustrations. Large 8vo, cloth, gilt. 15s. net.

MR. WALTER CRANE, in a lengthy review in the *Manchester Guardian*, wrote : ". . . To pack into a single volume of some 626 pages and 400 illustrations a really intelligible account of the styles of ornament prevailing in the world from prehistoric times to the middle of the nineteenth century is A REMARKABLE FEAT. . . . The illustrations are for the most part well chosen and characteristic, and are drawn with decision and facility."

PATTERN DESIGN
For Students, treating in a practical way the Anatomy, Planning, and Evolution of Repeated Ornament. By LEWIS F. DAY. Containing about 300 pages, and 300 practical Illustrations from specially prepared Drawings and Photographs of the Principles of Repeat Design, the "Drop," the "Spot" Geometrical Ornament, etc. New edition, revised and enlarged by AMOR FENN, with many fresh Illustrations. Demy 8vo, cloth, gilt, 10s. 6d. net.

"Every line and every illustration in this book should be studied carefully and continually by every one having any aspiration toward designing."—*The Decorator.*

ABSTRACT DESIGN
A Practical Manual on the Making of Pattern. By AMOR FENN, late Head of the Art Section, Goldsmith's College, New Cross. A series of careful, informative sections on Conditions, Elements, etc. Illustrated by about 180 full-page Designs from the Author's specially-prepared Drawings. 8vo, cloth, lettered. 12s. 6d. net.

ROUND THE WORLD IN FOLK TALES
A Regional Treatment. By RACHEL M. FLEMING. 16 Tales from Iceland, Mexico, Africa, Australia, etc., told in a fresh, easy style. With 17 Illustrations from Prints, Drawings, and Photographs. 8vo, boards, 2s. net. Cloth, 3s. net.

NATURE AND ORNAMENT

By Lewis F. Day. Nature the Raw Material of Design, treating chiefly of the decorative possibilities of Plant Form, its growth, features, and detail. With 350 Illustrations, chiefly grouped comparatively under Flowers, Seed Vessels, Fruits, Berries, etc., specially drawn by Miss J. Foord. New Edition, revised, with a Chapter by Mary Hogarth. Demy 8vo, cloth, lettered. 7s. 6d. net.

FLORAL FORMS IN HISTORIC DESIGN

Drawn by Lindsay P. Butterfield, Designer, with Introduction and Notes by W. G. Paulson Townsend. Containing 30 Plates in Collotype and Line, showing about 100 Decorative Adaptations of the Rose, Carnation, Fruit Blossom, etc., from Eastern and European stuffs, and from old Herbals. Large folio, in portfolio. 15s. net.

MODERN DECORATIVE ART IN ENGLAND

A Series of Illustrations of its Development and Characteristics, with Introductory Text by W. G. Paulson Townsend. Cheaper reissue. Large 4to, cloth, gilt. 12s. 6d. net.

TEXTILES, PRINTED FABRICS, WALL PAPERS, LACE AND EMBROIDERY, TAPESTRY, STENCILLING, BATIK, etc. Illustrating on 80 Plates 178 examples, including 51 subjects beautifully reproduced in full colour.

THE PRACTICAL DRAWING SERIES

DRAWING FOR ART STUDENTS AND ILLUSTRATORS

By Allen W. Seaby. Containing 220 pages, with 113 Illustrations printed in Sepia, mostly full-page Plates, from Drawings by Old and Modern Artists. Second Edition, revised and enlarged. Medium 8vo, cloth, paper sides. 10s. 6d. net.

COMPOSITION

An Analysis of the Principles of Pictorial Design. By Cyril C. Pearce, R.B.A. With chapters on Tone, Distribution, Gradation, Scale, Perspective, Rhythm, Harmony and Balance of Colour, Discords. Illustrated by 130 comparative and analytical Drawings, Sketches, and Diagrams, 6 Plates in colour, and 28 full-page Illustrations from Paintings by great Masters. Medium 8vo, cloth, gilt, paper sides. 10s. 6d. net.

PEN DRAWING

A Practical Manual on Materials, Technique, Style, Texture, etc. By G. M. Ellwood. Containing sections on History—Technique—Materials— Figures, Faces and Hands—Style and Methods—Landscape and Architecture—Modern Work—Magazine Illustration—Humorous Drawing Advertisements—Fashion. With numerous practical Diagrams by the Author, and 100 pages of Illustrations by the chief Pen Draughtsmen of present and recent times. Medium 8vo, cloth, gilt, paper sides. 10s. 6d. net.

THE ART OF DRAWING IN LEAD PENCIL

By Jasper Salwey, A.R.I.B.A. A Practical Manual dealing with Materials, Technique, Notes and Sketching, Building up, Form and Style, Process Reproduction, etc. Second Edition, revised and enlarged. Containing 232 pages with 122 finely printed reproductions of selected Pencil Drawings of Land and Seascapes. Figure-Studies, Book-Illustrations, etc. Medium 8vo, cloth, gilt, paper sides. 10s. 6d. net.

THE PRACTICAL DRAWING SERIES—(continued)

THE ART AND PRACTICE OF SKETCHING

A Comprehensive Treatise on the Practice of Sketching by every method. By JASPER SALWEY, A.R.I.B.A. The Author deals successively with varous media—Pen, Pencil, Water-colour, Oil, Wash, Crayon, Chalk, etc., and gives a complete account of the Technique of each. Illustrated by 64 Plates of half-tone illustration and 6 Plates in colour, with various Line Illustrations in the text from the work of great Masters. Medium 8vo, cloth, paper sides. 10s. 6d. net.

SKETCHING IN LEAD PENCIL

By JASPER SALWEY, A.R.I.B.A. An Introduction to the same author's "Art of Drawing in Lead Pencil," but dealing entirely with sketching as differentiated from the making of finished Drawings. A practical manual for the Architect, Student and Artist. Containing 111 pages and 56 Illustrations, by well-known artists in the medium, and by the author. Medium 8vo, cloth, gilt, paper sides. 7s. 6d. net.

ANIMAL ANATOMY AND DRAWING

By EDWIN NOBLE. Illustrated by a series of Plates in facsimile of the Author's Drawings of HORSES, CATTLE, DOGS, BIRDS, AND WILD ANIMALS, representing also Features, Details, etc. Including also numerous full-page and smaller Line Drawings of Anatomy, Muscles, Bones, etc. Medium 8vo, cloth, gilt, paper sides. 10s. 6d. net.

SKETCHING FROM NATURE

A Practical Treatise on the Principles of Pictorial Composition. By F. J. GLASS. CONTENTS: Choice of Subject and Planning of Sketch—Tones—Exercises in Composition—Examples from the Old Masters. With 6 Plates in colour and numerous composition from the Author's Drawings, and a series of Plates by Peter de Wint, Crome, Constable, Harpignies, Bonington, etc. Medium 8vo, cloth. 10s. 6d. net.

FASHION DRAWING AND DESIGN

By LOUIE E. CHADWICK. Illustrated by numerous examples of Historic Fashion Plates, Explanatory Sketches by the Author, Figure Studies, and a series of about 80 full-page and double Plates of Contemporary Fashion Drawings by well-known artists. Cheaper reissue. Large 8vo, cloth, lettered. 7s. 6d. net.

COLOUR : A MANUAL OF ITS STUDY AND PRACTICE

By H. BARRETT CARPENTER, late Headmaster of the School of Art, Rochdale. A Series of 16 concise but very practical chapters, based on the Author's experiments, on Harmony—Contrast—Discord—Keynotes—Intermingling—Effect of Lighting—Dirty Colour—Black-and-White, etc. Illustrated by 24 Plates (some double size), printed in colour; giving 40 Examples of Colour Combinations, Grading, Toning, etc., including some new examples of application in Historic Design. New and Revised Impression. 8vo, cloth, gilt. 9s. net.

"This book has been revised and enlarged, making it a treasure for all who wish to understand the value of colour. Like most of the books published by this house, the type is bold and clear and the many coloured illustrations are really beautiful. I feel this book will bring sunshine into the darkest day, and would recommend it to all."—Arts and Crafts Journal.

A COLOUR CHART

Issued in connection with the above book. Consisting of a circle 17 inches in diameter, printed in Graded Colour, showing 14 shades, Combinations and Contrasts. With explanatory letterpress. Folio, stout paper. 2s. 6d. net.

ART IN DAILY LIFE FOR YOUNG AND OLD

By D. D. SAWER. A comprehensive practical course for Teachers, Students, and Art Lovers; treating of the Place of Drawing, Plants and their Use, Figure Drawing and Drapery, Animal Drawing, Modelling Shapes and Figures, Casting, Clay Modelling, Object Drawing, Notes on Crafts, Composition, Design, applied and graphic. Each chapter is divided into three sections: A historical résumé, a note on educational significance and a briefer review of its practice and technique. With 10 Plates in Colour, and numerous full-page and text Illustrations in Line and Half-tone. Medium 8vo, cloth, lettered. 12s. 6d. net.

EVERYDAY ART AT SCHOOL AND HOME

By D. D. SAWER. A Practical Course based on the new Board of Education "Suggestions to Teachers," and adaptable to Dalton Methods, con taining graduated lessons on Brushwork, Design, Flower-painting, etc., with sections on Architectural Drawing, Lettering, Stained Glass, Leatherwork, and other Crafts. With 64 Plates in half-tone, from the Author's Drawings, numerous full-page and smaller Line Illustrations, and 8 Plates in colour, many Verse Extracts, etc. Medium 8vo, cloth. 12s. 6d. net.

PERSPECTIVE IN DRAWING

A simple Introductory Account. By Miss D. D. SAWER, late Art Lecturer at the Diocesan College, Brighton, Author of "Everyday Art at School and Home." With an Introduction by Professor ALLEN W. SEABY, Headmaster, School of Art, University of Reading. With Sections on Basic Principles, the Cube, Cylinder, Shadows, Reflections, Aerial Perspective, Colour, and Drawing. Illustrated by over 100 Diagrams and Sketches, a Frontispiece in colour, specially drawn by the Author, and reproductions from Photographs. Crown 8vo, cloth, 5s. net.

SKETCHING AND PAINTING FOR YOUNG AND OLD

An Elementary Practical Manual, by D. D. SAWER, late Art Mistress, Brighton Diocesan Training College, Author of "Everyday Art Perspective," etc. With chapters on: Ungathered Wealth, a Day Out, Materials, Practice, the First Sketch Out of Doors, Composition, Mounting and Framing. Illustrated by coloured Frontispiece, 8 Plates in Line and half-tone, and 31 text Illustrations from the Author's specially prepared Sketches, Diagrams, etc. Crown 8vo, stiff covers, 1s. 6d. net; or quarter-cloth, lettered, 2s. net.

THE ART OF THE BODY

Rhythmic Exercises for Health and Beauty. By MARGUERITE AGNIEL, Dancer and Physical Instructress. A series of simple, easy and enjoyable exercises, illustrated by numerous Photographic Plates, specially posed by the Author. With 100 subjects on 64 Plates, including many reproductions of dance poses and figure studies, draped and nude. CONTENTS: Function of the Spine—How to Walk Well—Figure Reducing—Exercises for the Digestive Organs, Back and Neck—Legs and Ankles—The Care of the Hands and Feet—Skin, Eyes and Teeth—Constipation—Women's Disorders, etc. Cheaper reissue. Large 8vo, cloth, gilt. 12s. 6d. net.

"For some years past I have been much interested in the ideas which Miss Marguerite Agniel not only advocates but so skilfully and delightfully embodies. By her own personal experiences she has been especially fitted to demonstrate the harmonious union of the æsthetic and hygienic aspects of physical exercise. There must be many to whom her work will prove fascinating and valuable."—HAVELOCK ELLIS

THE HUMAN FORM AND ITS USE IN ART

A Series of 118 Photographic Studies on 73 Plates from specially selected Female and Child Models, by F. R. YERBURY, including a Series of Male Studies by F. H. CROSSLEY, F.S.A. With an Introduction by G. M. ELLWOOD. Illustrated by 17 Photographic Plates and numerous Text Figures. With descriptive Notes on the Poses. Large 8vo, cloth. 18s. net.

LIVING SCULPTURE

A Record of Expression in the Human Figure by BERTRAM PARK and YVONNE GREGORY. With an historical and descriptive Introduction by G. MONTAGUE ELLWOOD. Comprising a Series of 47 full-page Studies of Selected Male and Female Figures with descriptive Notes. The Introduction is illustrated by 9 plates, giving 16 examples of the Human Form in Prehistoric, Greek, Renaissance and newest Art. Cheaper reissue. Small 4to, cloth, gilt. 12s. 6d. net.

LAUGHS AND SMILES and How to Draw Them. By A. A. BRAUN.

Containing 45 Plates, printed in tints of numerous constructional sketches, building up in successive stages humorous likenesses of well-known personages, and also figures from old Masters. Comprising in all about 300 Sketches by the Author, with concise instructive Text, including numerous anatomical Diagrams. Oblong 4to, decorative boards, cloth back. 3s. 6d. net.

"A book which young art students, or anyone with a practical taste for art, would appreciate. This attractive manual on humorous portrait-drawing should have a wide appeal."—*Overseas Daily Mail.*

FIGURES, FACES AND FOLDS

A Reference Book on Costume and the Female Countenance and Form. For Fashion Artists, Dress Designers, and Art Students. By ADOLPHE ARMAND BRAUN. Containing 112 comparative Plates, giving over 300 Illustrations of Costume and Drapery, and of typical Women's Faces, from antique statues and paintings. Including a special series of nude and draped studies from selected models specially posed for fashion work. With practical text, Dress diagrams, Figure details, Anatomy analysis, etc. Cheaper reissue. Demy 4to, stiff paper covers, 10s. 6d. net; cloth, gilt, 12s. 6d. net.

THE CHILD IN ART AND NATURE

By A. A. BRAUN. Containing chapters on Anatomy, Development, and Expression, and over 300 Illustrations from Photographs and Drawings of child poses, expressions, the Child Figure in Art. Second Edition, revised and enlarged. Cheaper reissue. 4to, in stiff covers, 10s. 6d. net; or cloth, gilt, 12s. 6d. net.

ALPHABETS, OLD AND NEW

With 224 complete Alphabets, 30 series of Numerals, many Ancient Dates, etc. Selected and Arranged by LEWIS F. DAY. With a short account of the Development of the Alphabet. Crown 8vo, cloth. 5s. net.

"A book which has, perhaps, proved more helpful than any ever before issued on the subject of alphabets."—*The Decorator.*

A valuable and attractive little Manual.

PEN PRACTICE

By WALTER HIGGINS. Chapters on Tools, Broad-pen Practice, Spacing, Italics, Uncials and Half-uncials, Setting out, A Cursive Hand, etc. With 27 Plates specially drawn by the Author, giving some hundreds of Letters, Ornaments and Exercises, and 6 from selected Historical Examples. Crown 8vo, stiff paper covers, 1s. 6d. net; or cloth, lettered, 2s. 6d. net.

THE ROMAN ALPHABET AND ITS DERIVATIVES

A large-sized Reproduction of the Alphabet of the Trajan Column. By ALLEN W. SEABY. A Series of large Plates, printed from the wood blocks, and including typical examples of Renaissance, Gothic, and Modern Alphabets and Types. With Introduction and descriptive Notes. Medium 4to, half-bound, lettered, or in portfolio. 4s. 6d. net.

DRAWING, DESIGN AND CRAFTWORK

For Teachers, Students, and Designers. By FREDK. J. GLASS. Containing 224 pages, with over 1750 Illustrations on 214 Plates, from Drawings by the Author. Third Edition, revised and enlarged with many new Plates. Demy 8vo, cloth. 12s. net.

MODELLING

A Practical Treatise for the Use of Students, etc. By F. J. GLASS. Containing Chapters on Modelling for Bronze, Wood, Stone, Terra-Cotta, etc; Modelling a Bust from Life; Figure Modelling; Relief Work; Composition; Casting; Gelatine Moulding; Proportionate Enlargement, etc. With an additional section on the History of Sculpture and Modelled Ornament. Illustrated by about 30 Plates of comparative stages and processes of Modelling, with about 35 Plates of the greatest Sculpture of all Periods, together with many Line Illustrations in the text. Royal 8vo, cloth, gilt. 15s. net.

ETCHING CRAFT

An Illustrated Guide for Students and Collectors. By W. P. ROBINS, R.E. With a Foreword by MARTIN HARDIE, Victoria and Albert Museum. Containing 250 pages on History, Technique, the work of the great Etchers, Dry-point, Aquatint, etc. Illustrated by 100 Plates of Etchings by Dürer, Rembrandt, Hollar, Whistler, Brangwyn, Clausen, Augustus John, Meryon, Forain, Zorn, and many other famous Etchers. Large 8vo, half-bound, gilt. 10s. 6d. net (formerly 21s. net).

PRACTICAL WOODCARVING

By ELEANOR ROWE. Third Edition, revised and enlarged, in Two Parts: I. ELEMENTARY WOODCARVING, embodying "Hints on Woodcarving." With numerous Illustrations, many full-page, from Drawings and Photographs of carving operations, examples and details. II. ADVANCED WOODCARVING. With numerous Illustrations, many full-page, from Drawings and Photographs of historic and modern carvings. Demy 8vo, limp cloth, lettered. 5s. net each; or two parts in one volume, cloth, gilt, 10s. net

ONE HUNDRED AND ONE THINGS FOR A BOY TO MAKE

By A. C. HORTH. With Notes on Workshop Practice and Processes, Tools, Joints, and full reliable directions for making Working Models. Illustrated by numerous full-page and smaller practical Diagrams and Sketches specially prepared. Second Edition, revised and enlarged. Crown 8vo, cloth. 5s. net.

DINNER BUILDING

A Book of entertaining and practical instruction in the Noble Arts of Cooking and Eating. Written by W. TEIGNMOUTH SHORE. With an Introduction by GILBERT FRANKAU. A series of 42 bright, stimulating but practical Talks on such subjects as The Perfect Dinner, Sandwichery, Remnant Days, Cabbages and Things, incorporating hundreds of fresh recipes of all kinds. Cheaper reissue. F'cap 8vo, cloth, lettered. 2s. net.

SAMPLERS AND STITCHES

A Handbook of the Embroiderer's Art. By MRS. ARCHIBALD CHRISTIE. Containing 34 full-page Reproductions from Photographs, a Frontispiece in colour, and 239 Text Drawings. Second Edition, revised and enlarged. Crown 4to, boards, canvas back. 25s. net.

ART IN NEEDLEWORK

A BOOK ABOUT EMBROIDERY. By LEWIS F. DAY and MARY BUCKLE. Fourth Edition, revised by MARY HOGARTH. Including a specially worked Series of Stitch-Samplers, numerous supplementary Diagrams and many Plates of Historic Embroidery—Chinese, Mediæval, Italian, French, and Modern English. With additional Examples of Modern Work by DUNCAN GRANT, MRS. NEWALL, MRS. STOLL, D. HAGER, and others. Containing 280 pages, 80 full-page Plates, reproduced from Photographs, and 50 Illustrations in the text. Crown 8vo, cloth. 7s. 6d. net.

SIMPLE STITCH PATTERNS FOR EMBROIDERY

By ANNE BRANDON-JONES. With coloured Frontispiece and 13 Photographic Plates illustrating 44 Patterns, 4 Plates from the Author's Pen Drawings, showing 31 Stitch Diagrams and 11 Complete Objects. With an Introduction, Chapters on the Method, Sketches, Colour Materials and Application of Designs, also descriptive Notes, with Colour Schemes. Crown 4to, paper wrappers, 2s. 6d. net; or in cloth, 3s. 6d.

"There is valuable help in this book. There are excellent plates in line and colour. The directions are clear and concise, and the articles suggested for practice are such as will please young people to make."—*Education Outlook.*

STITCH PATTERNS AND DESIGNS FOR EMBROIDERY

By ANNE BRANDON-JONES. An independent companion volume to the above work, containing 48 pages with 45 photographic examples on 12 Plates of simple and effective embroidery Motives, a Frontispiece in colour, and numerous Text Illustrations of Stitches and Methods. Crown 4to, paper wrappers, 3s. od. net; or in cloth, 4s. od. net.

CANVAS EMBROIDERY

A Manual for Students and Amateurs by LOUISA F. PESEL. Containing 48 pages of text, a coloured Frontispiece, and 14 specially prepared Plates showing Stitches and methods. Medium oblong 4to, paper wrappers, 3s. net; or bound in cloth, 4s. net.

ENGLISH EMBROIDERY. I. DOUBLE-RUNNING, OR BACK STITCH

By LOUISA F. PESEL. With coloured Frontispiece, 10 specially drawn Plates of 45 Working Designs, and 8 Plates from Photographs of 10 English and Coptic Samplers, comprising numerous Patterns and Motives. With Practical Text and a Preface by ETTA CAMPBELL, Embroidery Teacher, Winchester School of Arts. Uniform with "Canvas Embroidery." Large oblong 4to, paper wrappers, 3s. net; or boards, cloth back, 4s. net.

ENGLISH EMBROIDERY. II. CROSS-STITCH

By LOUISA F. PESEL. With a Coloured Frontispiece, 10 specially drawn Plates of 32 Working Designs, etc., and 8 Plates from Photographs of 15 typical English Samplers and Objects. Comprising 43 subjects, giving hundreds of Patterns and Motives. With Practical Text and a Preface by Professor R. GLEADOWE, late Slade Professor of Fine Arts, Oxford University. Large oblong 4to, paper wrappers, 3s. net; or boards, cloth back, 4s. net.

HISTORIC TEXTILE FABRICS

By RICHARD GLAZIER. Containing: Materials—The Loom—Pattern—Tapestries—Dyed and Printed Fabrics—Church Vestments, etc., with about 100 Plates from Photographs and from the Author's Drawings, including 4 in colour, and 43 Line Diagrams, illustrating over 200 varieties of Textile Design. Large 8vo, cloth, gilt. 21s. net.

ILLUSTRATED STITCHERY DECORATIONS

By WINIFRED M. CLARKE. Containing 19 Plates from the Author's specially prepared Drawings, giving some 120 useful original Motives: Borders, Rosettes, Floral Elements, Patterns, Lettering and Worked Objects, such as Bags, Blotters, etc. Including a coloured Frontispiece, Introductory Text and full descriptive Notes on the Plates. Crown 4to, stiff paper wrappers, 3s. net; boards, cloth back, 4s. net.

"A new and extremely useful little book for the embroidery worker. Miss Clarke has succeeded admirably in her task."—*Edinburgh Evening News.*

THE BOOK OF WEAVING

By ANNA NOTT SHOOK, U.S.A. Containing 190 pages, with 12 Plates in colour, comprising 34 Examples, and 31 Plates of about 130 Drawings, many in half-tone. Small 4to, cloth, lettered. 15s. net.

The aim of this work is to make the use of the handloom practicable and profitable in homes, schools, and institutions. The text is in 5 sections, on Weaving To-day and Yesterday, How to Weave, What to Weave, Art in Weaving (Design, Colour, Dyeing), Who Should Weave; with full information on equipment, processes and materials. The drawings show details of working and suggested designs, and the examples in colour are from pieces woven by the Author's pupils, such as tapestry, rugs, bags, cushion covers, shawls, scarves, etc.

THE ART AND CRAFT OF OLD LACE

In all Countries, from the XVIth to the Early XIXth Centuries. By ALFRED VON HENNEBERG. With an Introduction by WILHELM PINDER. Containing a full original account of the Development of Style and an Analysis of Technique and Texture. Including descriptive Notes and a Bibliography. Illustrated by 190 full-page Plates, 8 in colour, giving 60 specimens from scale diagrams and 250 of the finest pieces of Old Lace. Large 4to, cloth, gilt. £3 3s. net.

THE SMALLER HOUSE OF TO-DAY

By GORDON ALLEN, F.R.I.B.A., Winner of the *Daily Mail* Prize for the Best £1500 House. Containing Notes on Sites and Subsoils, Plans, Exteriors, Methods, Interiors, Hygiene, Gardens, Finance, etc. With 2 Plates in colour, 64 from Photographs, and 153 Illustrations from Line Drawings of Houses, Plans, and Designs. Medium 8vo, cloth. 10s. 6d. net.

THE CHEAP COTTAGE AND SMALL HOUSE

By J. GORDON ALLEN, F.R.I.B.A. New Edition, remodelled and enlarged, containing over 150 Illustrations from Drawings and Photographs of Cottages and their Plans, Housing Schemes, etc., from the latest Designs. Medium 8vo, cloth. 8s. 6d. net.

THE ART AND CRAFT OF HOME MAKING

A Comprehensive Guide with an Appendix of Household Recipes. By EDWARD W. GREGORY. Second Edition, revised, with additional Chapters and new Illustrations. Containing Practical Hints and Information on such subjects as Taking a House—Wallpapers—Furnishing Various Rooms — Pictures — Kitchen — Heating — Carpets — Curtains — Things that Get Out of Order—Costs, etc. Containing 224 pages, with 9 Plates in full colour of decorative schemes by GORDON BLUNT, numerous Photographs of Interiors by well-known architects, and many Sketches, Plans, and Diagrams in the text. Square 8vo, cloth lettered. 7s. 6d. net.

A BOOK OF BUNGALOWS AND MODERN HOMES

A series of Typical Designs and Plans. By CECIL J. H. KEELEY, F.S.I., A.R.San.I., Architect. Comprising 36 Designs, with large scale Plans, Brief Descriptions and Estimated Cost, including some Two-Storey Houses, Frontispiece in colour, Interior Views, Photographic Plates, etc. Large 8vo, cloth, lettered. 7s. 6d. net.

"The work may be recommended to those people who are on the look-out for homes designed with intelligence and convenience, and who have an eye for charm and artistic finish."—*Field.*

ARCHITECTURAL DRAWING, PERSPECTIVE AND RENDERING

By CYRIL A. FAREY, A.R.I.B.A., and A. TRYSTAN EDWARDS, A.R.I.B.A. Containing accounts of Measured Work Colouring, Sketching, Methods of Technique, Shading, Competition Drawings, Publicity and Posters, etc. Including a specially prepared Perspective in various stages by C. A. FAREY and Drawings by William Walcot, R.A., F. Brangwyn, R.A., W. Curtis Green, A.R.A., P. D. Hepworth, J. D. M. Harvey, and other well-known draughtsmen. With 43 Plates in half-tone, 9 in colour, 31 Line Reproductions, and 196 pages of Text. Cr. 4to, cloth. 16s. net.

ARCHITECTURAL DRAWING

By G. GORDON HAKE, F.R.I.B.A., and E. H. BUTTON, Architects. An Introductory Treatise for Architects and Students on Architectural Drawing of every type and in every medium. With 96 pages of text, 16 pages of Half-tone Illustrations and about 90 Line Illustrations in the text. Cheaper reissue. Medium 8vo, cloth. 7s. 6d. net.

"An excellent little book which every student should possess. The illustrations are uniformly good, and the general turn-out is of the high quality we expect from Batsford's." —*Illustrated Carpenter and Builder.*

FURNITURE FOR SMALL HOUSES

A Series of Designs. By PERCY A. WELLS. Containing 56 Plates reproduced from Photographs and Working Drawings by the Author, together with Illustrations in the text. Cheaper reissue. Small 4to, cloth. 7s. 6d. net.

"Mr. Wells's main concern is with the practical needs of a small house, and from this point of view his work is quite excellent. The photographs maintain the high standard which we associate with Messrs. Batsford's publications and the book should be read and studied by all who are interested in the long-awaited renascence of English cabinet-making."—*The Athenæum.*

HANDCRAFT IN WOOD AND METAL

A Handbook for the use of Teachers, Students, Craftsmen, and others. By JOHN HOOPER and ALFRED J. SHIRLEY. With over 300 Illustrations from Drawings and Photographs. Second Edition, revised and enlarged. Large 8vo, cloth, lettered. 10s. 6d. net.

CRAFTWORK IN METAL

A Practical Elementary Textbook for Teachers, Students, and Workers. By ALFRED J. SHIRLEY. Comprising a series of progressive Lessons and Exercises, illustrated by numerous full-page Plates from the Author's Drawings, each accompanied by detailed working directions, including also Practical Notes, Tables, etc. Medium 8vo, cloth. 5s. net.

"It bears the imprint of the successful practical teacher—hence its value to other teachers of the craft. We predict the book will be extensively used by teachers and students in the metalwork centres."—*The London Schoolmaster.*

SHOULD WE STOP TEACHING ART?

By C. R. ASHBEE. An interesting and outspoken account of modern Art Education. 8vo, boards, buckram back. 3s. 6d. net.

THE NEW MOVEMENT IN THE THEATRE

By LEÒN MOUSSINAC. With a Foreword by GORDON CRAIG. An elaborate International Survey of the Characteristics and Development of the Theatre in post-war Europe and America. With 120 Collotype Plates, comprising 250 figures and Costume Studies of which 115 are in colour. Also 235 Stage Settings, etc., many of them in colour. Introductory text translated and adapted by R. H. Packman. Thick Folio, buckram, gilt, £10 10s. net.

"I cannot praise this magnificent book too much. Its bountiful illustrations are the only way in which the stage developments of the last ten years could be conveyed. There can be no one who is connected with the theatre who would not get instruction and enjoyment from it."—*New Statesman*.

THE NEW STYLE

Architecture and Design. A Survey of its First Phase in Europe and America. With an Introduction adapted from the French of MAURICE CASTEELS, and descriptive notes on the Plates. Comprising 144 full-page Plates in Photogravure of Buildings, Interiors, Furniture, Lighting, etc., by well-known modern architects such as Le Corbusier, Mendelsohn, Gropius, Dudock, Mallet-Stevens, etc., chosen to illustrate the new movement in all its most representative manifestations. 4to, cloth, gilt. 12s. 6d. net.

THE NEW INTERIOR DECORATION

An Introduction to its Principles and International Survey of its Methods. By DOROTHY TODD and RATMOND MORTIMER. With over 200 Illustrations on 96 Plates of Interiors of every sort, Furniture, Carpets, Textiles, Lighting, Wall Painting, etc., of the new school by such Architects and Artists as Le Corbusier, Mallet-Stevens, Gropius, Oud, Duncan Grant, Lescaze, etc. With a frontispiece in colour from a drawing by E. McKNIGHT KAUFFER and full Introductory and Practical Text. Demy 4to, art canvas, with decorative wrapper by E. McKNIGHT KAUFFER. 12s. 6d. net.

MODERN THEATRES AND CINEMAS

By P. MORTON SHAND. A series of 80 plates giving over 100 examples of ex· teriors, interiors, foyers, vestibules, lighting, mural decoration, details, etc., of Theatres and Cinemas in the modern post-war style in France, Germany, England, Scandinavia, Italy, America, etc. Containing reproductions of the work of such architects as Margold, Kaufmann, Siclis, Gropius, Lipp, Ionides, Sauvage, de Soissons, Wilms, Mendelsohn, etc. Containing in addition numerous plans, elevations, sections in the text. Large 8vo, art canvas. 15s. net.

"A most interesting book; its illustrations are superb. You don't need to be an architect to enjoy reading this book. All you need is an intellectual curiosity into what is being done in the world to evolve new architectural forms. It is not only intensely interesting to read but it teaches you also what is going on in other countries."—*Tatler*.

REPRESENTATIVE BRITISH ARCHITECTS OF THE PRESENT DAY

By PROFESSOR C. H. REILLY, M.A., F.R.I.B.A., Director of the Liverpool School of Architecture, Author of "Recent Street Architecture," etc. An Account of Twelve Typical Distinguished Figures, their Careers and Work, including Professor Adshead, Robert Atkinson, Sir Herbert Baker, Sir R. Blomfield, A. J. Davis, E. Guy Dawber, Clough Williams-Ellis W. Curtis Green, H. V. Lanchester, Sir E. L. Lutyens, Sir Giles Gilbert Scott, and Walter Tapper. Illustrated by 80 Photographic Plates, including 12 Portraits, and Exterior and Interior Views of well-known Buildings. Large 8vo, cloth, gilt, 7s. 6d. net.

INDEX OF AUTHORS' NAMES

Made and Printed in Great Britain by The Stanhope Press Ltd, Rochester